Old men, young again ~ old men, young again /ur ma iguseda peibri pekem iguseda ~

Ali had the arms of a fisherman ~ the legs of a sailor ~ for so long a time he lived from the riches of the sea ~ working sunrise to sunset on the turn of tides ~ with hooks and lines and nets he made his living ~ once he was a young man ~ now he is an old man ~ but his eyes shine bright when he talks about the sea/and he caught with his hands ~ the fish that fed the islands ~ Ali Drummond is a young man when he talks about the sea ~

'Old Men And The Sea'
From *Island Way*, 2006
Seaman Dan, Karl Neuenfeldt &
Kyana-Lili Neuenfeldt Pearson

Life b'long Ali Drummond
A Life in the Torres Strait

Samantha Faulkner with Ali Drummond

Aboriginal Studies Press

First published in 2007
by Aboriginal Studies Press

© Samantha Faulkner & Ali Drummond 2007

Reprinted 2008

All rights reserved. No part of this book may be reproduced or transmitted in any form or by any means, electronic or mechanical, including photocopying, recording or by any information storage and retrieval system, without prior permission in writing from the publisher. The Australian *Copyright Act 1968* (the Act) allows a maximum of one chapter or 10 per cent of this book, whichever is the greater, to be photocopied by any educational institution for its education purposes provided that the educational institution (or body that administers it) has given a remuneration notice to Copyright Agency Limited (CAL) under the Act.

Aboriginal Studies Press
is the publishing arm of the
Australian Institute of Aboriginal
and Torres Strait Islander Studies.
GPO Box 553, Canberra, ACT 2601
Phone: (61 2) 6246 1183
Fax: (61 2) 6261 4288
Email: asp@aiatsis.gov.au
Web: www.aiatsis.gov.au/aboriginal_studies_press

National Library of Australia
Cataloguing-In-Publication data:

Faulkner, Samantha.
Life b'long Ali Drummond : a life in the Torres Strait.

ISBN 9780855755560 (pbk.).

1. Drummond, Ali, 1917– . 2. Drummond, Ali, 1917– — Family. 3. Torres Strait Islanders — Ethnozoology. 4. Torres Strait Islanders — Science. 5. Divers — Torres Strait — Biography. 6. World War, 1939–1945 — War work — Queensland — Torres Strait Islands. 7. Lawn bowlers — Queensland — Torres Strait Islands — Biography. 8. Torres Strait Islands (Qld.) — Social life and customs. I. Title.

920.00929915

Printed in Australia by Ligare Pty Ltd

Cover images: Ali during his pearling years; Aerial shot of Thursday Island, photo by George Serras, courtesy Torres Strait Regional Authority & National Museum of Australia. Shell illustration by James Boyd.

All songs reproduced with approval.

Contents

Acknowledgments
vii

Prologue
ix

Map
xx

Introduction, Donisha Duff
1

Young Days
3

Life on the Water
13

Wartime (1940–42)
43

Life on the Land
53

Family
61

And Now
79

Acknowledgments

Family is important to all of us. It is especially important to the Aboriginal and Torres Strait Islander communities. Our extended families provide support, guidance and leadership to individuals as well as continuing the strong oral tradition and transmission of culture from one generation to another.

Having a record of Ali Drummond's life is important to me: he's my grandfather. So it's also my family's story, as well as an opportunity to share his rich and varied experiences with a broader community.

I hope this book encourages other Aboriginal and Torres Strait Islander people to take the same journey; to record the history of our elders, families and communities for younger generations, and for all Australians to share.

I thank my mum, Vicky, for her valued assistance in shaping the stories that have been detailed throughout the book and my sister Donisha for providing the introduction, as well as her support and advice over the years. I thank my aunties: Cux, Bonnie, Teena, Dilly, Laura and Cindy, and Uncle Paul for contributing their memories and photos. This book has also been made possible with the involvement of all my extended family.

I also thank Alex Barlow for his patience, advice and guidance as a mentor over the years and the Australian Society of Authors, in particular the team behind the inaugural Indigenous Mentorship Scheme (2002). The Indigenous Mentorship Scheme provided me with the opportunity to develop the manuscript. I extend my thanks also to the Australian Institute for Aboriginal and Torres Strait Islander Studies (AIATSIS) for the initial research grant in 1998; this book would not have been possible without their support. Thanks also to Aboriginal Studies Press for their willingness to publish this story and their constructive comments and support with the manuscript.

I would like to thank my husband Warren for his patience, understanding and support. Without it I would never have accomplished this.

Finally, I thank Grandad for sharing his story with me in the first instance, and allowing others to hear it as well. I hope I have done it justice.

To you, the reader, I hope you enjoy this book. Grandad overcame adversity at a young age to achieve the things he has done. If there is a message in this book it would be to appreciate what you have, namely your family, and to remember that we all, each and every one of us, has a story to tell.

Samantha Faulkner

Prologue

The Torres Strait lies between the tip of Cape York in far north Queensland and the Island of Papua New Guinea, a distance of 150 km at the narrowest point. The waters and reefs that surround the islands are home to a range of ecosystems and include habitats for rare aquatic species.

Of the more than 100 islands in the Torres Strait, nineteen are inhabited. The total population of Torres Strait Islanders in the Strait is approximately 6900, while the total population of Torres Strait Islander people in Australia is estimated to be 48,800 which includes 19,600 people of Torres Strait and Aboriginal heritage. Of the total population, 45 per cent live in parts of Queensland outside the Torres Strait area and 18 per cent live in NSW (Census 2001 on http://www.reconciliation.org.au/i-cms.isp?page=292, accessed 21 June 2007). On the islands, populations vary between communities, but they number from between 70 to 750 people. There are twenty communities, including the Northern Peninsula Area, (Cape York, mainland), and each maintains a local council. Traditionally the village has been the basis of social organisation but Torres Strait Islanders may identify through their clan, village or island. They are diverse peoples with differing needs. The Torres Strait is part of Queensland and the Torres Strait Regional Authority provides administration over the area. The islands are grouped into the following clusters:

Top Western Islands (closest to New Guinea)
Boigu, Dauan, Saibi, running from west to east

Near Western Islands
Badu, Mabuiag, Moa — Kubin, St Pauls communities

Central Islands
Iama (Yam); Masig (Yorke); Poruma (Coconut); Warraber (Sue)

Eastern Islands
Mer (Murray); Ugar (Stephen); Erub (Darnley)

Inner Islands
Hammond; Muralug (Prince of Wales); Ngurupai (Horn); Thursday Island — TRAWQ (represents the residents of the suburbs of Tamwoy, Rose Hill, Aplin, Waiben and Quarantine on Thursday Island), Port Kennedy

Northern Peninsula Area
Bamaga; Seisia

Many Torres Strait Islanders live on their islands in the Torres Strait, while others (two-thirds) live in mainland Australia around Townsville and Cairns in northern Queensland and Darwin in the Northern Territory. Earlier generations of their families had been evacuated to the mainland in World War Two, and stayed there after the war. Many families moved south to the mainland seeking better employment opportunities.

Traditional lifestyles on the islands were shaped by the available resources. The western islanders were hunter–gatherers while the central and eastern islanders relied on the sea, and trade with other islands.

Being surrounded by the sea has shaped a unique Torres Strait life and culture, with historical descriptions of the Islanders by Europeans noting them as dextrous fishers and divers and formidable warriors. Fishing remains a strong part of the Islanders' way of life. This continued into the early twentieth century when diving for bêche de mer, trochus and pearl shell shaped the lives of many Islander men (and their families) who crewed the luggers.

Evidence of generations of close trading and cultural links with New Guinea are evident in the long drums, sometimes covered in shark-skin, and traditional dance costumes and masks used in performances in the Islands and on the mainland.

The fan-shape and white feathers of the 'dhari'/'dhoeri' headdress have become a symbol of the Torres Strait, with a stylised version incorporated in the Torres Strait flag. The flag provides a symbol of the unity and identity of all Torres Strait Islanders, and was designed by the late Bernard Namok. Some dhari include shark motifs, reflecting the Islanders' respect for the sea and their totems, while others incorporate models of planes from World War Two, a significant time for Torres Strait Islanders. Originally made from local materials like wood, fibre, leaves, feathers and shells; brightly painted wood, tin and plastic are also used. As well as being used in ceremonies, some dance costumes are collected by art galleries.

Each clan and island group have their own costumes and special performances, some of which are added to and enhanced for special occasions like the Coming of the Light Festival in July which celebrates the coming of Christianity to the islands. Thursday Island also hosts the Torres Strait Cultural Festival which is held every two years. Run now for many years, the Cultural Festival includes both Australian and overseas performers.

The Croc Festival is another time for coming together with the focus on encouraging young remote and rural Australians to lead healthy, positive lifestyles. Children from different Island communities, along with some from

Aboriginal communities from northern Queensland, join for days of celebrations with traditional and contemporary dancing.

Torres Strait Islanders continue to maintain their culture, while exploring new media in other artforms. The Gab Titui Cultural Centre on Thursday Island is a cultural keeping place and information centre, while the new Kubin Art Centre provides a source of economic and social activity. Torres Strait artists are expanding into new artforms like printmaking and are now exhibited in the Torres Strait and on the mainland.

Music too reflects Torres Strait Islanders traditional roots, as well as their collaborations with other musicians and adaptations of music from other traditions. Legendary singer and former diver, Uncle Seaman Dan, has won numerous music and cultural awards. Now a septuagenarian, Uncle Seaman Dan's recorded music includes songs from Oceania, Hawaii, Fiji and Norfolk Island. Rita Mills, one of the Mills Sisters, was also instrumental in keeping alive traditional Island songs. Better known to younger audiences, Christine Anu is a Cairns-born urban-style pop singer while Getano Bann performs original material which reflects his life experiences and mixed heritage.

Increasingly, Torres Strait Islanders are telling their stories in print, with biographies, autobiographies and novels, poetry and children's stories published by small and mainstream publishers. These complement the work of earlier collectors of traditional stories which have been published since the 1960s and 1970s. Such collectors, and communities themselves, now deposit their materials in collecting institutions on the mainland, some of which, like the Australian Institute of Aboriginal and Torres Strait Islander Studies (AIATSIS), digitise and repatriate materials to communities. Other Torres Strait Islanders are entering tertiary education and starting to take their place as educators and policy makers and advisers.

***

In sport too, Torres Strait Islanders have excelled. Douglas Pitt Jnr, famous as one of the best skin divers, and known as 'King of Malay Town' in Cairns, was presented with a medal from the Queensland government for rescuing people from drowning between 1899 and 1920. Danny Morseu has had an international career as a basketballer. However, it's in rugby league that Torres Strait Islanders have forged perhaps their strongest reputation as sportspeople. These include professionals Eric Pitt (Mossman) and Ted Mosby, Wendell Sailor, and Sam Thaiday who plays for the Brisbane Broncos.

***

Although many Australians know less about the Torres Strait than the mainland, Murray Island, or Mer as it is known by its custodians, rose to prominence in the public imagination with Eddie Koiki Mabo's challenge to the previously accepted notion of 'terra nullius'. This action saw its way to the High Court of Australia. Sadly for him and his family, he passed away too soon to see the fruits of a decade of activism and litigation by him and other Mer Islanders, take shape in the Mabo decision (*Mabo v Queensland [No. 2]*). On 3 June 1992 the Australian High Court ruled that the land title of Australia's Aboriginal and Torres Strait Islander peoples was recognised as common law, stemming from their rights over land which pre-dated European colonisation. It has proved a turning point in Australian history, if not its sense of identity, even though some of the early elation has disappeared as the ensuing native title legislation has delivered less than many Aboriginal and Torres Strait Islander Australians expected or hoped. Each year on 3 June, Torres Strait Islanders celebrate the High Court decision.

***

Western scientists now believe that the Torres Strait Islands, as we know them now, took shape about 2500 years ago. From the beginning, Torres Strait Islanders valued their independence, but since the landing of European people, Torres Strait Islanders have had to work hard to remedy the effects of 150 years of paternalism and injustice, including the effects of the 1880s Haddon Expedition from Cambridge. Some of the Expedition's reports were published in the early twentieth century, and their influence in shaping governmental control and education has been pervasive.

Linguists believe that the languages spoken in the Torres Strait indicate both Melanesian and Aboriginal influences and structures. Meriam Mir (derived from Papuan languages) is spoken in the Eastern Torres Strait, while Kalaw Lagaw Ya is spoken on the western, central and northern islands. In both cases, individual dialects are found on each of the islands. Yumiplatok (Torres Strait Creole) has developed over time. It is a mixture of the two traditional languages and English. It is now the most common language in the Torres Strait, and in towns on upper Cape York and some towns on the east cost of northern Queensland. For most Islanders, English may be their second or third language with English being taught to all school students.

***

Living on myriad islands in a large stretch of water, Torres Strait Islanders' maritime focus is reflected in their lives spent living off the sea, for example, hunting dugong and turtles. While much is made of the Torres Strait as a bridge to mainland Australia (traditionally a hunter–

gatherer society), from Papua New Guinea (traditionally a horticultural society), Torres Strait Islanders have developed a lifestyle and unique cultural traditions that reflect their identification with the sea.

The Torres Strait Islanders traded with other communities and cultures for years: the eastern and western islanders with New Guinea, while the southern islanders traded with the Aboriginal people of Cape York. The Islanders seafaring skills and their ocean-going canoes (often in small fleets) allowed them to travel far afield. However, it was the English seamen passing through the Torres Strait (Captain James Cook in 1770, followed by Captain William Bligh and Midshipman Matthew Flinders) that was to change their lives forever. Captain Cook first claimed British sovereignty over the eastern part of Australia in 1770 at Possession Island in the Torres Strait. The local Kaurareg people, whose name for their home is Bedanug, were to gain native titles rights over their island and nearby islands in 2001.

Earlier voyages in the early 1600s were made by the Dutch and Spanish but it was the Spanish captain, Luis Vaez de Torres, after whom Europeans named the strait. Thus began the Islanders' first battle for their islands and waterways.

By the late nineteenth century traffic through the Torres Strait was frequent. The potential to exploit the sea's resources was evident and seekers of trochus, bêche de mer and pearls followed. Some were respectful of the Islanders' way of life. Through intermarriage, their descendants still live in the Strait. This included seamen from the Philippines and Japan who settled on Thursday Island. Japanese divers firmly embedded themselves in the pearling industry and this continued until World War

Two. However, not all visitors to the Strait were respectful; some acted extremely ruthlessly.

In 1879 the *Queensland Coast Inlands Act 1879 (Qld)* extended the control of the colony of Queensland to within a few hundred metres of New Guinea, effectively taking in all the islands in the Torres Strait. This followed on from the 1859 creation of the colony of Queensland.

At this time the Torres Strait Islander people lost much: control over freedom of movement (Islanders were confined to their islands), employment (the government had created a large, cheap labour pool), cultural observances (superintendants and protectors interfered with the Islanders' traditional culture of self-management and reciprocity), and opportunities for education (Islander children were educated to a lesser standard than those on the mainland).

Another influx of people to the islands of the Strait were the London Missionary Society (LMS) led by the Rev. Samuel Macfarlane. They arrived on Erub (Darnley Island) in the east of the Torres Strait in 1871. Their aim was to use the islands of the Torres Strait as a stepping off point in their efforts to evangelise further afield. Two years later they established the first Torres Strait school. The LMS was officially replaced by the Church of England which opened its Torres Strait Mission in 1915. The Church of England conducted services on Thursday Island from the late 1870s, while the Catholic and Presbyterian churches were built in the mid-1880s. Until the emergence of other Christian faiths after World War Two, many Torres Strait Islanders were part of the Church of England.

Some, though not all, Islanders welcomed the missionaries, as they afforded protection from armed European seamen. Ultimately the Islanders adopted the missionaries' Christian teachings, within a relatively short period, though they didn't completely abandon all of their traditional culture. Christianity remains strong in the islands today. The Coming of the Light which celebrates the first Christian religious service on 1 July 1871 and the coming of Christianity to the Torres Strait, is remembered each year with a church service, dancing and feasting.

The *Aboriginals Protection and Restriction of the Sale of Opium Act 1908 (Qld)* controlled the fates of Aboriginal people in Queensland — and Torres Strait Islander peoples — throughout much of the 20th century. It was the model for similar 'protective' and restrictive legislation in other Australian states, particularly those with high Aboriginal and Torres Strait Islander populations. As well as controlling opium, the Act restricted the movement of Aboriginal and Torres Strait Islander people, created cheap labour pools and stripped them of civil rights, making them, effectively, state wards.

***

World War Two was to have previously unimaginable effects on the islands. The perceived Japanese threat to Australia through the Torres Strait in the early 1940s led to the recruitment of segregated Torres Strait military companies. As the war came closer men were taken from their homes and co-opted to the war effort. More than 800 Torres Strait Islanders, including almost every able-bodied man from the outer islands, served in the defence forces in some capacity. Despite this contribution their underpayment of wages (originally one third of the European rate) wasn't finally compensated until 1987. In early 1942 Torres Strait Islander women and children were evacuated from Thursday and Hammond Islands to the mainland, though not the outer island communities. Many were to remain on the mainland, with their families, after the war ended. Poorly resourced coast watchers were sent to the larger island communities and these formed the Islanders' only protection. For those remaining, the only protection against the Japanese planes and bombings was to hide. Wartime rationing made life difficult, however, with the changes that war creates, some women were trained as nurses, with Ellie Loban Gaffney emerging as the first qualified nursing sister.

***

Torres Strait Islanders' expectations of a new way of life post-war, after having defended their country, were not to be met. A post-war boom in pearling fell away, and governmental paternalism and racism were rife.

The *Aborigines and Torres Strait Islanders (Land Holding) Act (Qld)* became law in June 1985 which granted land holdings to all fifteen of the Torres Strait Islands where people lived, except for Mer (Murray Island) which was the subject of the case being fought by Eddie Koiki Mabo and others before the High Court.

The Islanders' proximity to Papua New Guinea became significant when the latter gained independence in 1975. The people of the Torres Strait maintained their identity as Australians which led to government concern in Papua New Guinea about total Australian control of the strait's waters.

A deal was struck. The Torres Strait Treaty was signed in December 1978, though negotiations had begun earlier, in 1973. Ratification took place in 1985. The maritime frontier between Papua New Guinea and Australia runs through the strait and both countries cooperate in the resources found there, and recognise the traditional cultural practices of people.

Today the TSRA aims to improve the lives of Torres Strait Islanders and Aboriginal people living in the region. Their programs focus on addressing the poor socioeconomic and health outcomes of people, trying to overcome decades of disadvantage. The goal of self-determination is based on the 'Ailan Kastom bilong Torres Strait' and includes recognition of people's customs and identity; improving Islanders' quality of life; developing a sound and sustainable economic base; providing health and community services and protecting the environment.

The TSRA, first established in 1994, has an elected arm (twenty elected representatives who are Torres Strait Islanders or Aboriginal people living in the Torres Strait) and an administrative arm.

***

The Torres Strait region is one of the most diverse areas within Australia. Today, people of many cultures live and work in the Strait. The lifestyle is relaxed, with many people living by 'island time'. Torres Strait Islanders (especially those living on their islands in the Strait) have adapted: to years of paternalistic governmental policies, to a fluctuating economy, to the coming of a new religion, Christianity, to migration to the mainland to escape the war and to seek work. Throughout, they have withstood their encounters with the colonisers and held their culture strong.

Tourism is emerging as a new industry. It represents one way for the Torres Strait Islanders to develop economically viable industries which can be substituted for governmental assistance and provide the opportunity for self-determination. Others relate to access to the sea and marine resources, as well as petroleum exploration.

***

The Torres Strait is a beautiful place that many people call home. One legend tells it that if you eat the wongai fruit (native plum) you'll return to the islands some day.

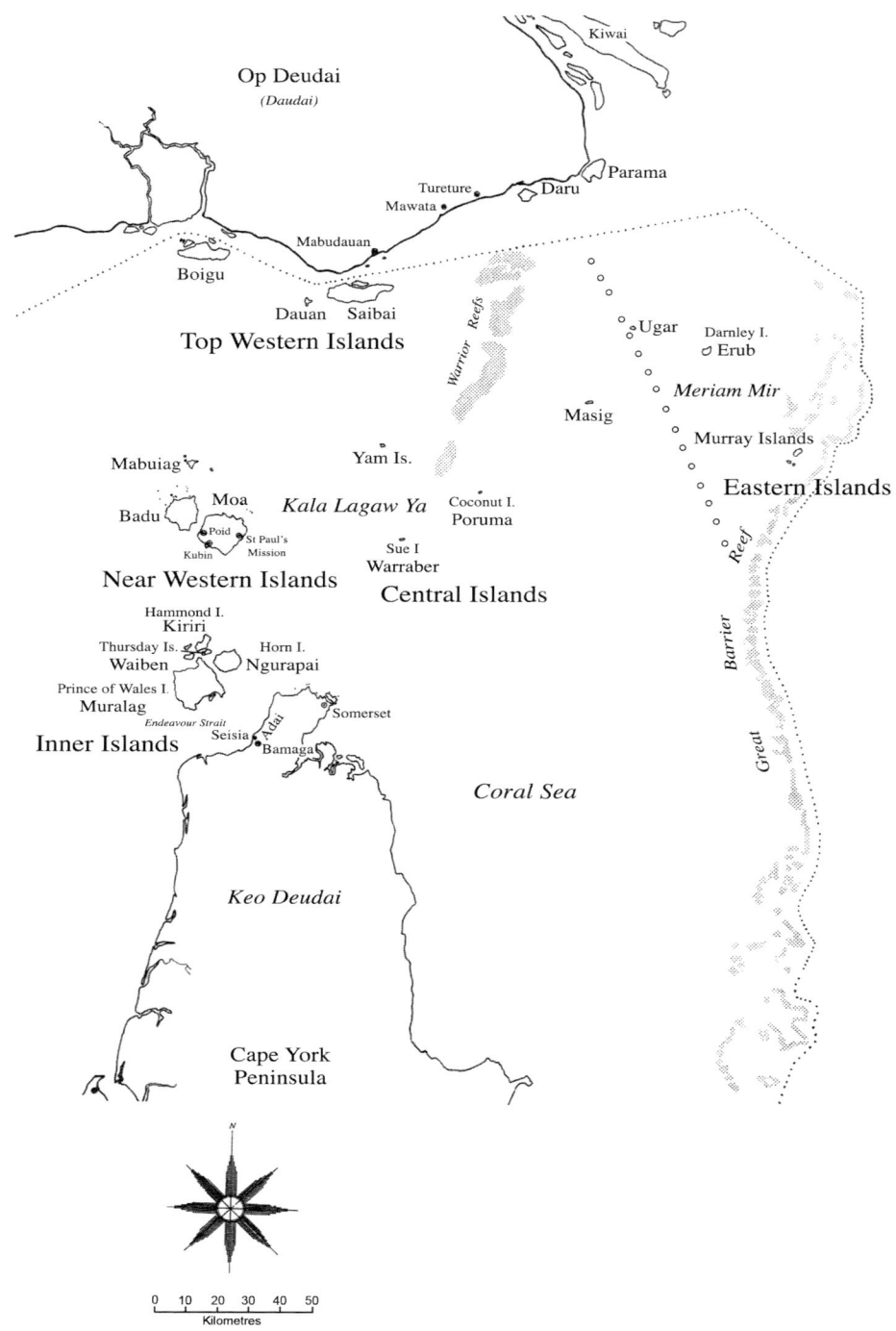

Islands of the Torres Strait and their neighborhood. Drawn by John Waddingham. Reproduced with permission from © Sharp, N, *No Ordinary Judgement*, 1996, Aboriginal Studies Press.

Introduction

It was mid-morning. The sun was shining down brightly and there was barely a whisper of wind. I sat on an upturned bucket in the middle of my Grandpop's 16-foot aluminium dinghy. He once told me that it was better this way so the weight in the boat would be more balanced. The man in question was standing up at the back of the boat steering the outboard motor.

As we turned the corner around the back of Thursday Island (TI) Grandpop continued his narration about his pearling experiences. He told of how the ocean floor was like a garden — really clear in some places, with shells and an assortment of debris lying around. I had to listen closely as every second word was drowned out by the hum of the motor. Grandpop continued to talk about the reefs that surround TI.

As I sat on the bucket straining to listen I saw a big brown patch thirty metres ahead on the sandy bottom. As we steered closer, I realised it was a huge boulder. I called out to Grandpop, 'stone there'. However Grandpop was so caught up telling me about the reefs and fishing around TI, he failed to hear me, and we ran straight over the top of it!

The boat scrapped against the rock and the outboard motor kicked up out of the water. Grandpop was surprised and 'growled' me for not looking out and telling him.

Introduction

I told him I'd said, 'stone there', but he was too involved with his story. 'Anyway,' I said, 'I thought you said you knew this place. You just spent the last four hours telling me!' With that, we both laughed. It was just a typical day with Grandpop.

Donisha Duff

Young Days

Why are you looking so sad my dear? ~ Why are you looking so blue? ~ Are you thinking of someone so far away? ~ In a beautiful place called TI ~

Old TI my beautiful home ~ It's the place where I was born ~ Where the moon and stars that shine makes me longing for home ~ Old TI my beautiful home ~

Take me across the sea ~ Over the deep blue sea ~ Darling won't you take me ~ Back to my home TI ~

TI my beautiful home ~ TI my home sweet home ~ I'll be there forever the sun is sinking, goodbye

        Old TI , public domain, attributed to Jaffa Ah Mat

Mohammed Ali Drummond was born on 17 July 1917, to Mohammed Drummond (also known as Drummond Sarawak) and Cissie Malay of Thursday Island (TI). Ali was born in a time when the Queensland government took control over the islands of the Torres Strait from the London Missionary Society. Aboriginal and Torres Strait Islander people were recognised as wards of the state and came under the *Aboriginals Protection and Restriction of the Sale of Opium Act 1908 (Qld)*. Reserves were formed and Aboriginal and Torres Strait Islander peoples were segregated from the rest of the world. Protectors controlled the affairs of Aboriginal and Torres Strait Islander Australians.

As there was no hospital on TI in the early twentieth century, a midwife delivered Ali at his parent's house on Victoria Parade which was next to the house known as the *Four Winds*, and just a short distance from the engineers' wharf. His birth certificate records his name as Mohammed Ali Drummond (after his father), but he was to become better known to everyone later in life as 'Ali'.

Ali's father was from the Dayak people of Sarawak, Indonesia, previously known as the Malay State. He came to Australia from Singapore in the early 1900s to work as a pearl shell diver in the then booming pearl and trochus shell industry. Many other Southeast Asian men were also employed as pearl shell divers and as crew on luggers at that time.

Ali's father was known on TI as 'Drummond Sarawak'. It was a Malay tradition to be called by your surname first and then the town where your family originated from. Little is known about Ali's Malay background, however, it is believed that the Drummond Sarawak family connection still exists in Indonesia.

After a long and often dangerous career of pearl shell diving, Ali's father turned to labouring and handyman jobs. In 1916, he met and married Cissie Malay. Ali's father had to apply for permission from the Protector to marry Cissie because she was designated as a half-caste Aboriginal woman and under the age of 21. Cissie and her father, Jimmy Malay, both consented to the marriage, but the Chief Protector of South Brisbane (William Lee Bryce) refused the application based on the age difference between the two. Jimmy Malay wrote to Chief Protector JW Bleakley in support of Drummond's application. In late October, Bleakley advised that the marriage was opposed. Despite that, in July 1917 Ali was born. Chief Protectors had the power to move people onto and between reserves and to hold children in dormitories and the Torres Strait was administered from Brisbane.

Cissie was the third daughter of Jimmy Malay (also know as Jimmy Goentjoel) from Java in Indonesia and Nara Para from Red Island off Cape York. Cissie's other sisters were Tidja, Jaima, Dahlia and Jessie. Jimmy Malay was of a Malay background as his name reveals. Nara Para was an Aboriginal woman from the Yadhaigana people, Shelburne Bay on Cape York Peninsula, along the east coast of northern Queensland.

Ali was the eldest son of Mohammed Drummond and Cissie Malay. Ali's siblings include Dahlia, Osman, Mary, Leah, and Jessie (Timmy).

***

Ali was raised on Thursday Island during a time when the population comprised peoples of diverse and culturally rich backgrounds. Ali remembers that Malaysian, Chinese, Anglo-Saxon, Philippine and Japanese people were just some of the many nationalities living on Thursday Island in the 1930s. Many Papua New Guinea people were employed as crew members on pearling luggers as they were recognised as cheap labour. Ali remembers some of the Papua New Guinea crew lived in boarding houses near the beach close by Ali's house.

Prior to World War Two there were no Torres Strait Islanders living on Thursday Island. Rather, they lived on the outer islands and came under the jurisdiction of the Protector and the Queensland Department of Native Affairs. It was only after World War Two, along with the recognition of the contribution that Torres Strait Islanders made during the war, that Torres Strait Islanders were allowed to live on Thursday Island. However, it wasn't without restrictions: Torres Strait Islanders had a curfew after 6pm and were not allowed to be on Thursday Island after that time. Instead, many of the Torres Strait Islander pearl shell crew slept on the luggers at night.

Ali's family were classified as Malay and were allowed to live on TI and were therefore not subject to the same restrictions as Torres Strait Islanders.

Ali began school when he was about five years old, right where the current primary school stands today. Ali said that his school 'was only for black kids', and that 'white kids went to a separate school'. The 'black' children included locals who were of Malay, Chinese, Philippine and Japanese backgrounds. The 'white' children's school was located near the old high school on Hargrave Street.

Ali remembers that 'schoolwork was basic with a rough and ready attitude'. The educational policy at the time encouraged Aboriginal and Torres Strait Islander children to continue only to a Grade 4 equivalent. Ali received a rudimentary education in arithmetic, English, the alphabet, and how to sign his name, and there was no homework. At school he enjoyed meeting his friends and playing games like marbles, cricket and football during the lunch break. Ali attended school until he was 14 years old, and completed a grade 6 education.

Ali said he 'grew up as normal as possible compared to everyone else'. His family moved later to a house at the back of where the Video 2000 shop is located on Douglas Street today. They lived close by their neighbours. A laneway led to Ali's house and fronting the laneway were some shops. The laneway led on further, to a well, with houses on either side. Ali enjoyed his childhood, going to school and playing with his friends. At the same time, his father taught him how to fish and over the years he spent a lot of time fishing from a sailing boat in the waters around Thursday Island. However, as the eldest boy he also had a number of household chores to complete.

Each day, Ali would rise at about 4am. His day would begin with a walk to the wharf at the main jetty. It took him about 15 minutes to walk the kilometre and Ali joined many others, mostly older people. There, in the good weather, he'd go fishing for dinner. Most of the time he managed to catch something, but he'd stay out until the sun came up. Ali's father taught him how to tell the time by the sun by measuring the distance between the horizon and the sun from his thumb to his middle finger. This measurement was roughly one hour. At about 8am, he would quickly gut and scale his fish, go home for a quick wash, get dressed for school and have a breakfast of bread with jam before heading off for school.

After school, he'd go home and then set out again, fishing until sunset. For dinner his family would eat fish. What they didn't eat for dinner, they'd salt and save to eat on another day. The family usually ate their fish with rice, damper or scone as fresh fruit and vegetables were not plentiful.

Ali's other household chores included carrying water from the communal well to fill the empty drums at the back of the house and collecting firewood from the beach. His brother, Osman (Bully) would sometimes help. However, Bully was his father's favourite son, because he looked like him in appearance. Ali's father told Ali what to do and if he didn't do what he was told, as Ali tells it, 'I would get a flogging'.

Ali spent a lot of his free time fishing, often going out to Blue Fish Point on Prince of Wales Island. This was one of his favourite fishing spots. He'd catch the easterly tide to and from Blue Fish Point, either rowing or sailing over. He usually fished with a cotton line and black hooks, similar to a kirby fish hook. For bait he used sardines or crabs which his father had caught the previous day.

Other times in the afternoon, Ali would catch crayfish, fish and squid with his friends Starchy Ah Wang, Ali Ah Mat and Peter Adams. They would go at low tide to the back of Thursday Island and fish between Thursday Island and Deadman Island where the crayfish were plentiful. Each would carry a one-prong spear and swimming mask. They'd stay there till sunset then go back home with the crayfish, fish and/or squid they caught for the evening meal.

Jarfar Ah Wang (Starchy's older brother) sometimes took Starchy, Ali Ah Mat, Jias Ah Mat and Ali in his 18-foot sailing boat (5.4 metres) to catch dugong near Channel Rock. Once Jarfar took the boys to a lagoon at the back of Thursday Island to try some dried crushed roots his Papua

New Guinean friends had given him. He told the boys to go to either side of the lagoon, then Jarfar went to the entrance and took a handful of the dried roots. He soaked the bundle a bit to soften it, then crushed it against the rocks so the juice from the dried roots could spread into the lagoon. It took about five minutes before the fish rose to the surface in a drugged state. They caught enough fish that day to share their dinner between the four of them.

Ali remembers a Chinese merchant called Sang Kee, who had a shop opposite the picture show. Sang Kee sold Asian and English goods during the day and in the evenings he cooked and sold 'long soup', a Chinese dish of chicken and noodles.

Ali (back row, far right) and friends after catching a small dugong, Thursday Island, 1930.

Sometimes during the week after school Ali and Peter Adams did some casual work for Sang Kee. They'd be told how many chickens to catch from the pen in Sang Kee's backyard, then they'd kill and clean them ready for cooking that evening. A small bowl of long soup cost one shilling and six pence and a large bowl was two shillings and six pence (about $7.90 in today's money). Both boys worked till about 9.30pm and were given a small bowl of long soup for their dinner and one shilling and sixpence or two shillings ($6.30), depending on how good business had been that night.

Ali's father was the provider for the family. His father had stayed working in pearl shell diving until he was forced to retire due to old age. Upon retirement, he worked as a handyman and as assistant to the local butcher, Mr Riley. Ali's mother stayed at home to look after the family and Ali remembers her as 'the boss of the household'. Ali's family had no radio and television hadn't even been invented. Ali said, 'the radio was only for the upper class'.

Ali's father was a practising Muslim and one Ali's earliest memories is that of his father praying. Ali would watch, fascinated, as his father went about his preparations. His father would put out a prayer mat and put on the Muslim head covering, the 'kufi', ready for prayers. His mother would chase Ali away so that his father could pray undisturbed. Although both his parents were adherents to the Muslim faith, Ali was not taught their religion.

Ali's father was actively involved with the Thursday Island community and surrounding areas. Despite being Muslim, Ali's father made a significant contribution to the Catholic Church. Drummond Sarawak and Victor McGrath built the first Catholic Church on Hammond Island. It was only a small church, but together they contributed their time and built it slowly, by hand.

Ali recalls that in those days the Catholic Church conducted their masses in Latin. The Catholic Church on Thursday Island (Sacred Heart Mission) was formed in 1884 under the Vicariate Apostolic of Melanesia and Micronesia, which included Papua New Guinea, as well as the Gilbert Islands, now known as Kiribati. The TI Sacred Heart Mission was transferred to the Diocese of Darwin in 1938. From there it expanded and a diocese was established in Cairns. Ali said that 'when this move was made to Cairns the mass was changed to English' and the TI Catholic Church was transferred to the Diocese of Cairns.

Sadly for the family, in 1931 Ali's father passed away. He had a bad case of dysentery from which he didn't recover. Within forty days of his father passing away more tragedy was to visit the family. Ali's mother passed away from a severe asthma attack. Ali, their oldest child, was just 14 years old. With no parents, his aunties (mother's sisters) took care of the children. Tidja (now Adams) took Bully, Leah and Mary, and Dahlia (now Bin Hoosen) looked after Ali, Jessie and Dahlia. Having lost both parents, Ali wasn't happy with the new arrangements, which meant he was apart from his siblings. As pearling luggers often employed young boys as crew members, Ali left to join the crew of a lugger where he slept and spent most of his time. This was to be the start of a long career on the waters of the Torres Strait.

Life on the Water

Diving down to forty fathoms at the Darnley Deep ~ Searching for the precious pearl shell the pearls to keep ~

All aboard the pearling lugger ~ Grafton by name ~ crews are waiting for the divers ~ praying for some rain ~

Goodbye to you farewell my love ~ Soon we'll be sailing to the Darnley Deep ~ And in your heart please think of me ~ for I'll come back to you from the Darnley Deep

Diving down to forty fathoms ~ Down deep below ~ How to find the precious pearl shell only divers know ~ I can see the other diver work here with me ~ Getting shells at forty fathoms in the Darnley Deep

Sailing home for dear Old TI ~ Divers all asleep ~ So we bid farewell to the Darnley Deep

Forty Fathoms
Henry (Seaman) Dan [Hot Music]

With the death of both his parents, life changed direction dramatically for Ali. After he left school, he found work as a casual crew member on the *Haku*, a lugger with Cleveland Pearling Company. The only options for employment at that time for young men were pearling, or fishing for bêche de mer (sea cucumber and close relative of the sea urchin; also called 'trepang') and trochus. Ali decided to follow in his father's footsteps and become a pearl shell diver. Trochus are large, conical-shaped marine snails found in shallow tropical reefs. Their mottled red–green and white shells contain a thick inner layer of mother-of-pearl (nacre). This was highly valued in the making of buttons until replaced by other materials, and in jewellery.

Pearling had become a boom industry in the Torres Strait around the late 1800s and early 1900s and Ali's father had been a pearl shell diver, working the 'old ground', the area west of Badu Island and near Warrior Reefs.

Ali's father had neither encouraged nor discouraged him from being a pearl shell diver. His brother, Bully, was later to try diving after World War II, but he didn't remain in the industry. However, Ali was willing to learn and worked closely with the Japanese pearl shell divers. He was to work hard and refine his skills and stay in the industry for many years.

It was during shore leave from pearl shell diving that Ali met and courted his 'first and only love' — Carmen Villafor. It was a whirlwind courtship that saw Ali and Carmen marry during his next shore leave. As they were both under 21, permission was required for them to marry. But there was to be no honeymoon: Ali returned to the lugger the following morning after marrying Carmen in 1936.

In his early days of pearling Ali met Thomo-San, a Japanese pearl shell diver who was to have a significant impact on Ali's life. Thomo-San became his mentor, passing on 'life's lessons' to the young Ali and showing him how to be a successful pearl shell diver. Thomo-San taught the orphaned Ali the value of money: 'to not spend it all at once, to save it and keep some aside for a rainy day'. Ali received basic wages when he first started pearling, which amounted to about three pounds and five shillings a month (about $228.70 in today's money). He saved most of his money by depositing his salary in the bank and living frugally.

Ali's father had many friends who looked out for him. One friend was Bargo Ah Mat, a pearl shell sorter with the Cleveland Pearling Company. Bargo was one of the divers who had come to Australia with Ali's father. He later married and settled on Thursday Island.

Ali's life on the water saw him working on a range of vessels, never staying too long on any one vessel. Over time, the area Ali covered as a pearl shell diver ranged from Darnley Deeps in the east to Bobo Island, Daru Island, Bristle Island near Papua New Guinea to the north, and Arukun, Mapoon, Crab Island and Brilliant Point.

Japanese divers and Papua New Guinean men crewed the *Haku* where he worked for the three months of the neap tide, weak tides that occur during quarter moons. From March to May he joined the lugger *Jogen,* part of the Carpenter fleet, as a casual crew member, and from June to August the lugger *Zena* and finally, the Bowden Pearling Company as a crew member. He was the casual cook of the *Sedney* for two years. Ali worked his way from apprentice to second then first diver, later becoming a skipper himself. Ali says that at the time 'he was young, daring and stupid'.

After his second year with the Bowden Pearling Company he left pearl shell diving to try collecting trochus and bêche de mer on the *Cuckoo*. The following year he went back to pearl shell diving as a second diver for the Hocking Pearling Company on the *Goose*. Ali moved between pearl shell diving and collecting trochus and bêche de mer, depending on the season, as did the other seamen. A season later he moved to another lugger in the Hocking fleet, the *Penguin*. The crews of both *Penguin* and *Goose* were Malaysian divers, with Papua New Guinean crew members. Through his working life in pearling Ali made many friends. He enjoyed and respected their friendships and recalls warmly now how his life was enriched by these relationships.

Life was also adventurous. Ali tells a story of a strange incident on the *Cuckoo*. They were working with another lugger on the reefs somewhere between Lizard Island and Cooktown on the Great Barrier Reef. The crew went out in dinghies at low tide and raced each other to the lagoons to look for trochus shell — three to four men in each dinghy. Ali was in a dinghy with Peter Adams, George Hollingsworth and Songhie Mills. In all, there were eight dinghies working that part of the reef.

At low tide the sea forms lagoons and exposes the reef, ideal conditions for collecting trochus shell. The men walked around the exposed reef, picking up any shell that they found, 'dry picking', instead of diving into the lagoons. When the tide came in again they headed back to their dinghies to return to the luggers, as the reef became covered in deep water.

Ali and his crew noticed one deep lagoon where the divers made speedy exits in their dinghies, having retrieved no shells. One crew after the other arrived and the same thing happened. The divers went in looking for trochus shell and left in a hurry, empty-handed.

By now Ali and his crew were curious. They followed the men and questioned them. The men replied that 'there was something big and black down there that came out towards them'. The crew hadn't waited around to find out what it was: they just jumped out of the water.

When Ali's dinghy reached the lagoon everyone in the boat jumped in. Before anyone had time to look for trochus shell, they saw a big dark shape coming towards them. None of the divers waited around to see what it was. They all headed back to the lugger as quickly as they could.

Later, on board the *Cuckoo*, the crew compared stories. None of the crews ever found out what was in there; they were in too much of a hurry to get out. They all had a good laugh and decided it must have been a big groper. Ali's crew didn't go back to the lagoon but they'd managed to fill an empty 44-gallon (200 litre) kerosene drum with trochus shell, so everyone was happy.

Ali remembers that during this time the waters of the Great Barrier Reef were clean and clear. You could see to a depth of two to three fathoms (about 5.5 metres). Beyond that the waters became too deep to see anything. You jumped in expecting to hit the bottom but you just kept on going down.

The Reef was a good spot for collecting bêche de mer. The season began in June/July and the luggers would unload their cargo in Cairns, then move on to collect trochus shell from September to December. At the end of December they'd sail home and then sign up crew for the next season.

Ali recalls another, more dangerous incident when he was working along the Great Barrier Reef. The crew had been working their way north along the Reef, collecting trochus shell, when they were hit by the tail of a cyclone.

The lugger rocked from side to side in the wind and fierce waves lashed the hull. Two anchors were dropped overboard but the boat didn't hold; the anchors dragged along the bottom of the ocean floor. The crew took turns to pump out the seawater as the waves washed over the boat. They started pumping after 1am and didn't finish till about 4.30am. The crew were fearful. A few men picked out objects to hold onto if the lugger sank; others were on the deck praying. Ali said 'You couldn't look out the front, the water was like having pebbles thrown at you.'

The Nobby at sea in 1948

However, Ali was confident that the skipper was experienced enough and would see them through this ordeal. By early morning, after a night of pumping, the seas calmed and the wind steadied. In the daylight they saw they were opposite Green Island, going from Stanford and Elford Reef to Arlington Reef. Ahead they saw what they thought was a reef. However, it was moving, and surfacing slowly. When they were about twenty to thirty feet away (6 to 9 metres), they saw that it was a whaler shark which they reckoned was as long as the lugger when they saw it swim alongside them. The men believed the whaler shark had come into shelter from the cyclone too.

***

When the luggers were out at sea the crew would eat mostly fresh seafood: fish, turtle, dugong and fresh seafood. Their meals were supplemented by anything they came across, or traded. As cook, Ali would prepare rice and miso soup for the Japanese divers. When they were in port he'd cook meat. The lugger's rations included two five-kilogram drums of plain flour, three five-kilogram bags of rice, tin meat, tin goods (including butter, jam, dripping, baking powder, condensed milk, salt, golden syrup, tea coffee and sugar), tobacco papers and matches, onions and potatoes. The luggers also carried a first aid kit made up of bandages, aspirin, iodine, Epsom salts, Japanese plaster and seasick pills.

Before the neap tide, the Japanese divers would buy a large basket of Chinese cabbage and turnips. Once back on board they'd separate the cabbage leaves, wash and salt both the cabbage and turnip and pack them in an empty wooden case. At sea during meal times they'd take out the vegetables, wash off the salt and slice them ready to eat.

On the way out to the pearling grounds the luggers would sometimes call into Nagir Island (Mount Ernest) for a few hours to visit old Frank Mills and his family. They gave him a bag of rice and a drum of flour and in return he'd give them the fresh produce they lacked: watermelons, young coconuts and any other vegetables he had growing in his garden. Fresh fruit and vegetables were rare at sea so they took any opportunity to trade with nearby islanders.

During the spring tide the crew would anchor at one of the islands, waiting for the next neap tide. Sometimes they'd go ashore to trade their rice and flour with the Islanders for fresh produce. Islanders on Yorke Island gave them bananas, sweet potatoes and dried wongai fruit, whereas Darnley Island was the main port of call for fresh water and a good shower.

Shellmeat was also eaten and often made into a curry. The shellmeat guts were used to make 'shokra', a before-dinner appetiser. Lemon, sugar, salt and vinegar were added to shellmeat guts in a bottle and the bottle was shaken once or twice a day. When it was ready to eat, the men would use wire bent into a hook shape to remove the shellmeat.

Ali learned his cooking from watching others. He would make his own yeast mixture for home-made bread. He would add rice grains, sugar, seawater and chopped potato pieces in a bottle. He made the mixture in the morning, bottled it and left it till the evening. However, he would shake it several times during the day. He would replace the rice grains during the week or make a new mixture.

For breakfast Ali would make soup, sometimes adding salted fish and bread during the day. Pancake and soups were also regular crew favourites. The lugger would lower a towline (a fishing line thrown overboard as the lugger was moving) during the day to catch seafood.

For dinner, Ali would fry fish to serve with bread and butter and a cup of tea. They seldom ate tinned meat and there was no refrigeration. 'It was rough and ready in those days,' Ali remembers.

The majority of divers at the time were Japanese. Ali remembers they came from working-class backgrounds, hence their ethic of hard work and not wanting to waste food. 'A good cook would give you a good meal and make sure you didn't starve,' Ali said.

One day when the *Sedney* called into Murray Island for a few days Ali was invited to have tea with Payo Mabo and family. They ate freshly caught sardines for tea and Ali was intrigued as to how the flesh could be peeled off the fish without any of the bones being removed.

The ladies had cooked the sardines in salty water so Ali thought he'd try that method and see what happened. The next day Ali took his cast net and caught a bucketful of sardines. Back on board the *Sedney*, he put the sardines in a big saucepan of boiling salted water. He was unsure of the cooking time and over-cooked them; they were mushy and fell apart when he tried to eat them.

Ali threw all the sardines away and went ashore to ask the ladies how to cook them properly. The Mabo family had a good laugh when he told them what had happened. He was told to boil the water, add the sardines, then stir the fish around and allow them to settle. When their eyes turned white, they were cooked and ready to eat.

Another time, on a lugger with Papua New Guinean crew, Torres Strait pigeon was being prepared for dinner. The pigeons were caught and kept alive until dinner. The young chicks just about to fly were the most tender to eat. The cook took the pigeons, hit their head on a bench to kill them and cut their neck. On seeing this one of the Malay men loudly disagreed with this method. He drew his knife, grabbed one of the pigeons, said a quiet prayer and then slit its neck. He killed the remainder of the pigeons for dinner that evening.

***

Prior to World War II it was mostly Japanese who dived for pearl shell although there were Malay and Polynesia men and some Torres Strait Islander men. They would just skin dive in shallow water and there were no women divers on the company boats.

Most of the men on the pearling luggers had family on Thursday Island or the outer islands and only when the luggers came in to port could they see their families. There were no maps or charts to use in those days. Navigation was done by the stars, tides and weather.

The luggers could be out at sea for anywhere from six to seven weeks at a time, depending on the weather. The weather, and finding a 'good bottom' were the determining factors to a successful time at sea. However, Ali remembers that 'The Japanese worked in all kinds of weather. Even if the weather was rough on top, as long as the water was clear they worked. They were hard workers.'

After two years at sea, it was on the *Sedney* that Ali learnt to dive. The chief or number one diver was Thomo-san, who took Ali under his wing in this as in other lessons in life.

At the Darnley Deeps, an area just off Darnley Island, the dive was about 32 feet (9.7 metres) without reaching the ocean floor. The crew would drop the leadline to determine the depth. The water there was cold, with nothing swimming around.

The divers would hang in an empty space and it took an hour to stage. If their bodies shook they knew they wouldn't get the bends. As Ali describes it, the bends were 'like ants crawling all over you then it hits you — "boom" all of a sudden. You would only regain conscious when someone staged you, and you were like a yoyo going up and down'. The 'bends' or decompression illness occurs when divers surface too quickly. Under water, at pressure, nitrogen is forced into the bloodstream. If divers ascend too quickly, not allowing time to 'off gas', nitrogen bubbles form leading to blotchy rashes, coughing spasms, dizziness, unconsciousness and an inability to bend the joints. On the surface, the nitrogen in the air is inhaled and exhaled without ill-effect.

Most divers didn't know the art of staging. Panic killed them mostly, or the watersnakes. They'd hold their breath getting to the surface instead of breathing out along the way up. Their lungs would burst when they reached the surface.

Ali was taught how to combat the bends by the Japanese divers. 'If you weren't feeling well after a dive and could feel the bends coming on, you stripped naked and put your feet in a bucket of water. Then you got the cold back in your body.' The Japanese men did it and he just copied them.

King-san, skipper and chief diver on the Bowden Pearling Company's *Minerva*, was thought to have developed the art of 'staging'. In turn, he'd taught other Japanese divers. He also developed the helmet (tin hat) and corselet for diving.

Ali remembers when King-san passed away. It was believed he had a heart attack going down at the Darnley Deeps. Unable to make any contact with him, the tender raised the alarm when he pulled up an empty helmet. King-san was missing for five to six hours. The *Sedney* stopped working and went to help the *Minerva* look for the missing diver. Both luggers dropped anchor and a diver from each lugger went below.

Engi-san, the second diver on the *Sedney*, found Kingsan's body and signalled for it to be pulled up. Ali helped the tender pull up Engi-san who was holding the body. A dinghy from the *Minerva,* came over to collect

Kingsan's body. The *Minerva*, flying half-mast, headed for Thursday Island with the other luggers following in a funeral procession. King-san was buried in the Japanese section of the Thursday Island cemetery.

***

Usually, just before dark, the divers came up to the surface after pearling and got ready to sail home unless they'd struck a 'good bottom'. When it darkened in the evening, the bottom of the ocean floor became lighter. Going down to the bottom, it became dark in the middle and then lighter at the bottom. Ali would remember the places he dived, and the position of the moon, tide and the wind. The Japanese divers kept diaries to record the places they dived.

Unloading shell from the Nobby *at Thursday Island Engineers Wharf, 1949*

There were different rope signals for different luggers. Ali remembers the signals which were as follows: 1: come up; 2: more air; 3: slack pipe line (air line), take in the slack/increase tension; 4: bag full; 5: bag up; 6: put marker buoy out; and 7: plenty fish.

***

Ali worked as number one diver for four years, both prior to and after World War II. The job carried a lot of responsibility as he had to find a good bottom and check on the weather. The old people would say to watch the sunset. If it was red that indicated a hot next day. If cockroaches flew around at night it would be windy in a couple of days and rough weather was expected. If you were working about 30 to 40 miles off Badu Island and that happened you'd head for home.

Ali remembers few bad days when he couldn't find any pearl shell. He used his brains and even if they had to scratch around a bit they always found some. The luggers would follow the 'neap'; the clear water. There were no favourite or horrible places to dive. Ali saw only sharks and turtles, but no mermaids!

When working in deeper waters, Ali remembers that the seabed looked like a beautiful garden, with pearl shells scattered everywhere. When he was growing up, he'd been told by the old people that every place had a keeper or guardian, even at sea. He was a visitor there, and as a mark of respect he should always ask permission to take some pearl shell, and when he had collected sufficient to say 'thank you'. Ali never forgot this practice and today his children carry on this tradition. Wherever they travel, they always ask permission when visiting a certain area and always say 'thank you' when they leave. This tradition of respect is always spoken softly.

There were many dangers when diving; some they expected, others they didn't. One time Ali saw two pearl shells nearby each other. However, given the drift of the tide, he calculated he'd miss one of them. He called for slack, more rope, to reach the shell further away from him. With the drift, he thought he'd still be able to reach the second shell. In his haste he accidentally stuck his fingers inside the open pearl shell and it closed on him. However, he went on and picked up the other pearl shell and put it in his shell basket.

When he came to the end of the patch his bag was almost full so he signalled to be pulled up. As he was surfacing he tried to release his fingers but the shell clamped down even tighter. The pressure intensified as he rose. He broke the surface and made it to the deck of the boat where he called for someone to bring him a knife. By this time his hand was white. A knife was inserted to open the shell and his hand was freed. Despite the pain, he still maintained his sense of humour, laughing that there was no pearl inside the pearl shell, even after the effort and danger he'd been through.

Ali took a year leave from pearl shell diving to spend with Carmen and his young daughter, Carmen Alexia. Ali and Carmen had started to build a family which would grow to include five daughters and two sons. See Family, p. 61.

***

After time away from the luggers, the following year Ali approached Don Farquahr of Farquahr's Pearling Company for a job. He was employed as skipper/number one diver of the lugger *Pearls*. By now Ali was 21. The remainder of the crew on *Pearls* consisted of Kara Kaprisi as second diver, two tenders, a cook, engineer and two crew.

Since becoming skipper and head diver Ali learned to notice the first signs of the bends and to take measures to avoid this happening.

Ali's first trip as skipper on *Pearls* was working with a fleet of luggers along the east coast of Queensland. The fleet were working in the main shipping passage and every now and then, they had to move out of the way of the big ships.

Despite his caution, Ali first got the bends working at Margaret Bay near Cape Grenville. He was one of the divers working at a depth of 10 to 12 fathoms (18 to 21 metres) and picking up good pearl shells. That evening after tea, Ali went over to the *Penguin* to see the skipper, Murphy Sullivan, to discuss where they'd be working the next day. While he was sitting down and talking, he suddenly noticed the lamp was blinking — an early sign of an attack of the bends. He lost consciousness. The next thing he remembered was waking up in a diving suit below the surface with another diver staging him. He signalled to the other diver that he was okay and to go up. Ali staged himself for another two hours. Reflecting on it later, Ali realised that he must have surfaced too quickly earlier on that day.

Ali remembers needing to be watchful of the weather, too. The *Pearls'* second trip down the east coast was as far as Flinders Islands near Princess Charlotte Bay. Another lugger *Wimble* from Hocking Pearling Company, skippered by Frances Sabatino, was working with them.

Both luggers were working on a good bottom in the main passage when a storm approached. This was the same area where another pearling fleet had been destroyed by a cyclone in 1899. The *Pearls* crew stopped working and went to shelter close to shore as they'd already collected one ton (.90 tonnes) of pearl shell. The crew on the *Wimble* continued working. It was very rough and windy when the storm hit. A dinghy came from the *Wimble* asking *Pearls* to accompany them back to TI because during the storm the *Wimble's* foremast had been struck and damaged by lightning, so after a quick repair job, both luggers left for home. When they reached Animal Island, just off Newcastle Bay, about 40 miles from TI, the *Wimble* stopped to work but *Pearls* continued on.

***

Diving held a number of dangers, some more expected than others. Ali recalls another tale of diving for pearl shell. Three divers, Mickey Seden, Bully Drummond (Ali's brother) and Willy Missi were out. There was a long drift, and the men were far from the boat. On deck the crew were concerned because they saw lots of bubbles and the divers signalled for more air. Suddenly, without warning, the three men surfaced and got straight out of the water, all at once. They took Willy Missi's helmet off, but Bully couldn't wait and came out of the water with his helmet still on. There'd been a big shark swimming around in the water, so the divers had surfaced in a hurry, eager to be out of the water in case the shark returned.

***

Ali never lost a diver when he was skipper but he came very close to losing his own life. The incident happened when he was on the *Whyalla*, from 1951 to 1952, the last years of his pearl shell diving career. He was working near the top end of Warrior Reef, not far from Tudu Reef.

Ali was diving off the stern of the boat and was working at a depth of about 16 to 17 fathoms (28 to 30 metres), when he found a good bottom. He had almost filled his shell basket when he signalled for more air. His tender acknowledged but a minute or two later Ali was still waiting for fresh air. Ali signalled again for more air and to be pulled up. Again his tender replied but Ali was still not getting any fresh air.

By now the air in his helmet was quite stale so Ali thought, 'This is it. Something is wrong with my airline. I'll have to throw my helmet and try to get to the surface for fresh air.' The way the airline and the lifeline was lying in the water, Ali thought the easiest way to the surface would be straight up. Just then the tender started to pull on his lifeline. Ali threw his helmet and started to swim up towards the surface. He didn't panic and on the way up he slowly swallowed seawater to cool his burning chest.

The crew became alarmed when only an empty helmet came up. Meanwhile they'd discovered that Ali's airline was caught around the boat's propellor. They knew he would be coming to the surface and were watching out for him.

Ali surfaced about 100 metres from the boat and called for them to hurry up and get him — he was tired and was finding it hard to tread water. In their haste the crew tipped over the dinghy in the water and lost a paddle. They eventually got to him and as they pulled him into the dinghy the saltwater he had swallowed started pouring out of his nose and mouth. Ali was exhausted and could feel his heart pounding.

Back on board the boat he was very angry and told the crew, especially his tender, that their carelessness had almost cost him his life. He'd earlier told his tender how to position the boat and to make sure to keep the airline clear from the stern of the boat. The exact two things the tender failed to do. Ali told them to cut and clear the airline from the propellor and then sail for Mangrove Island for the night. They later found that the piece of airline they cut from the propellor was twisted and flat.

The next day Ali took his turn diving and felt a lot better afterwards. When the *Whyalla* arrived in Thursday Island Ali went to the hospital for a medical check-up. His doctor found there was still nitrogen in his blood so he prescribed some liquid medicine to help disperse it properly.

Reflecting on what happened to him that day, Ali thought that he'd been saved because he hadn't panicked: he'd swallowed saltwater to keep cool, and he'd worn a raincoat jacket for extra warmth when working below – this had helped him to the surface and kept him afloat.

Another time on the *Whyalla* his tender acted quickly to prevent Ali from what he believed to be danger. They were working near the main passage along the east coast of Queensland, Ali wasn't far from the wreck of the *Quetta*. He wanted to see what she was like and how she was lying

Pearling on the Nobby, *Cairns, July 1949*

on the bottom. As he got closer to the wreck, his tender pulled him up. Ali was disappointed, but found out later that his tender thought he might get tangled in the wreck, and pulled him up to be well clear of the shipwreck.

A tender's role is important in the working life of a pearl shell diver. When the diver is below looking for pearl shell, his tender lowers him just a few feet off the bottom so that he can save his energy and drift along with the current, until he comes across a patch of pearl shells. The diver then signalled for his tender to lower him to the bottom to pick up the pearl shells.

***

In 1939 Ali was skipper and number one diver on the lugger *Charm*. His second diver was Jacky Smoke. The other crew consisted of two tenders, a cook, an engineer and two crew.

That season the *Charm* was one of the many luggers working near Bobo Island. It was a neap tide, clear and still, with a depth of about 14–15 fathoms (about 27 metres). Ali was working on a bottom where the edges would just drop into the ocean and he describes it now as like working on a table top.

The *Charm* followed the neap to start work just west of Deliverance Island. Ali and his second diver were working at 10–12 fathoms (about 18 to 19 metres) and picking up first-class pearl shells. They found the bottom was different to the old ground at Badu, as there was more mud and this produced shells that were thinner and lighter. They started diving that morning and at about 3pm, when the lugger was going back to do another drift, Ali again got the bends.

A helmet was put on the unconscious Ali and he was put back into the water with another diver to stage him. It was near 10 fathoms (18 metres) when he regained consciousness. As soon as he started to feel better he signalled to the other diver to return to the surface. It was not until six hours later, that Ali was safely back on board.

The *Charm* also had a close call with a patrol boat in the waters off Papua New Guinea. Ali was picking up good quality pearl shells when his tender signalled him to come up. Ali did not want to go up but his tender started to pull him up. Ali was angry as he was not ready to come up. When he reached the surface his tender explained that a patrol boat had spotted them and was coming towards them.

The patrol boat must have had a diesel motor because the black smoke from the exhaust gave them away. Ali quickly told the crew to start the engine and to head back into Australian waters. With a good easterly wind behind them they soon caught up with some other luggers working very close to the border. They also stopped working and headed for Kemos Reef.

About two hours later all the luggers were safely in Kemos Reef. The patrol boat went amongst the fleet of luggers with a loudspeaker warning them never to cross the border again, because 'if we catch you, your boat will be confiscated and the crew will be sent to prison'. After that excitement some of the luggers went to Mangrove Island while the *Charm* moved on to work elsewhere.

***

When the luggers anchored in Aragon Bay at Badu Island to shelter from the weather, the crew would get together and have a singalong. The lugger crews would be out to seas for weeks at a time. There were about ten men of various ages and ethnic backgrounds and because they had to sleep, eat, dive, work and share a small space, it was important for them to get along when working, and relaxing.

Some of the popular songs of the time were 'Goodbye to you, my Nona Manis', 'Red Sails in the Sunset' and 'Out on the Ocean' (a song made up by Kitchell Ano and friends). 'Red Sails in the Sunset' was a particular favourite of Ali's. Whenever he was feeling lonely, he would sing it.

Goodbye My Love, My Nona Manis
by Danny Everett and friends

Goodbye to you my Nona Manis
Don't you forget
Jangan la lupa kepada saya

But in your heart you will always think of me
Say ada mimkpi kepada sayang

But I'll return, my Nona Manis
Wait for me
Jangan la lupa kepada saya

If in your heart, you always think of me
Saya ada tumbah la dari
Sweetheart

Out on the ocean

Out on the ocean
That has no end
That's where we work
And that's where we play

The wind is so strong
We can't get along
So we set sail again
For TI

Nobody cares for me
There in TI
Nobody cares if I live or die
For I'm just a lonely seaman

And nobody loves me
I'm out on the ocean
Where there's no woman
On the ocean that has no end.

Pearly Shells

Pearly shells, pearly shells
From the ocean, from the ocean
Shining in the sun, shining in the sun
Covering the shore, covering the shore.

When I see them, when I see them
My heart tells me that I love you
More than all those little pearly shells

For every grain of sand upon the beach
I've got a kiss for you
And I've got more let over for every star
That twinkles in the blue

Pearly shells, pearly shells
From the ocean, from the ocean
Shining in the sun, shining in the sun
Covering the shore, covering the shore.

When I see them, when I see them
My heart tells me that I love you
More than all those little pearly shells

***

Pre-World War II, the pearl shell divers wore a full suit which comprised a rubber suit, heavy boots, tin helmet and corselet. Post-war it was a lot cheaper and easier to work in sandshoes, flannel pants and shirt and the tin helmet and corselet.

The glass on the front of the tin helmet (viewing glass) was fitted last, just before the diver went over the side of the boat. This viewing glass was one inch thick (2.5cm) and had to be stored separately from the rest of the diving equipment. It was cleaned regularly with a spoonful of coffee grains wrapped in a wet flannelette cloth. A dirty glass could cause the diver to have double vision and lead to a serious accident.

***

Ali left pearling in about 1940 to join the Civilian Construction Corporation, based on Thursday Island during World War Two. (See Wartime, p. 43). Later he worked on the mainland cutting cane. (See Life on the Land, p. 53). In late 1947, when Ali was in Cairns, Kara Kaprice asked if he was interested in going back to pearl shell diving. Ali thought about it and went to Cairns staying with his sister Dahlia and family. In July 1948, he went back to pearling on the *Nobby*, a lugger with the Schimafanny Company.

***

During the post-war pearling, Ali noticed that the same men came back again to pearl shell diving. The ocean floor had also a chance to replenish. With the Japanese interned on Thursday Island during the war, only those Japanese men married to Australian women were allowed to stay. The remaining Japanese men were sent back to Japan.

On the *Nobby* in 1948, Ali collected nearly 4 tons (3.5 tonnes) during good weather on a neap tide. The most pearl shell he ever collected was just over 24 tons

(22 tonnes) for five months' work during the season. He received $1100 (in today's money) for one season. He'd gone into partnership with Micky Sedan, his brother-in-law, and together they earned $2200. They were paid by cheque and finished the season. Most of the crew finished the season (May to December) and were paid on Thursday Island where they signed on. Post-war Ali, as skipper of the lugger, was paid 40 per cent of the earnings of the season while 60 per cent went to the owner of the lugger.

***

When Ali found a good bottom he would put down a marker buoy. Over the years, he used many different types of marker buoys. He used a dry coconut from Mabuaig Island and tied it to a piece of bamboo cane. This marker

Ali during his pearling years, August 1950

was successful because the other luggers thought it was just a coconut drifting with the ocean currents.

One time on the *Nobby* he struck a good bottom on the way out to the old ground. He used an empty fuel drum as a marker and continued working. Another lugger came along, found the marker and stopped to pick up what they thought was a good drum. They soon discovered that this was Ali's marker so they started to work there too. Before long there were several luggers working the area alongside the boat.

Ali decided to change his marker buoys. However, after working that area for four days he estimated that he found two tons (1.8 tonnes) of pearl shell. They worked for another four to five days and collected just over three tons (2.7 tonnes) of pearl shell, which filled fifteen pearl shell cases. Each pearl shell case weighed one cut (one hundred weight, or 50.8 kilograms). During another good neap Ali collected three and a half tons (3.18 tonnes) of pearl shell. For some divers, the record for the season was five and a half tons (4.98 tonnes). For others, it was between 15 to 20 tons (13.6 to 18.14 tonnes). Ali's record was 22 ton (19.95 tonnes).

The *Nobby* worked from July to December. Bob Mcdonald, the Aboriginal cook, would make johnny cakes for breakfast, served with syrup and damper. Ali would drink coffee too, as this would warm him up. During the day, they'd work a section of the bottom, then come out of the water and eat while the boat went back to the original section. They would work the same ground for the day, back and forth.

The *Nobby* had two divers: Ali who was both skipper and number one diver and Micky Seden who was the second diver. Both divers worked from sunrise to sometimes late at night. Depending on the weather, and if there was a good shell patch they worked on into the night, cleaning and preparing the pearl shells for their arrival back in port on Thursday Island.

***

Ali never lost a diver when he was skipper, but other skippers weren't so lucky, or careful. Divers on other boats died of the bends and were buried on Darnley Island. On all the small islands from Darnley to Thursday Island lie divers' graves, there being no medical checks at the time to determine the cause of death. An island lava-lava, a man's wrap around clothing for the lower half of the body, was used as a flag to let the other luggers know of the death of a diver. If the lava-lava was flown at half mast on the fore mast it would indicate the death of a forehead or middle diver. If it was flown at the main mast it would indicate the death of the stern diver/skipper.

***

During his time working on the *Nobby* Ali was almost involved in a brawl. One day he came ashore at Thursday Island and left the crew on the boat to unload the pearl shell and check on the rations. He went up to the Grand Hotel for a beer and was having his second beer, when three men started yarning and bragging very loudly. They were saying that they were in the Torres Strait during the war and that everyone else was 'akan', frightened or scared, to fight the Japanese. They said to Ali 'you akan, because you run away', referring to when everyone was evacuated.

Ali looked around to see who they were talking to and realised that they were talking to him. He became very angry, so angry that his right hand shook. He was so wild with rage he could barely hold his beer and remain composed. The other men continued to antagonise him by repeating the accusation.

Eventually Ali could not take it any longer, he stood up turned around and said, 'Fuck off! Where were you in the war? Well where were you? Answer me that.' Ali, of course had been a vital part of the war effort (see Wartime, p. 43). The men in the bar were surprised and taken aback at his outburst. Slowly, and apologetically the men left the bar. Just then Ali's brother Bully and Micky Seden came in. They noticed he was very upset and asked what was wrong. When Ali told them what had just happened, Bully got angry and wanted to go after them but Ali said not to worry about it.

Another day when Ali and another Malayan called Julianus (Paman Julie) went to the Federal Hotel in Cairns for a drink. The bar attendant told them that Torres Strait Islanders were banned from drinking there because they'd caused some trouble earlier in the month. Some men posing as Torres Strait Islanders had caused the trouble. There was a Malayan ship in port at that particular time and because Ali and Julianus were conversing in Malay, the bar attendant served them thinking they were from that ship.

A few months after joining the *Nobby*, Ali almost got the bends. He had to remove his helmet while ascending quickly to the surface from the ocean floor. From this recent incident he was found to have nitrogen in his blood. At this time, the family flew from Cairns to Thursday Island to be with him and eventually stayed there.

In another incident on the *Nobby*, Ali saved a Japanese diver's life. Ali was working on the old ground, with Badu Island in the distance, 60 to 70 miles (about 104 kilometres) away. The old pearling ground was 6–8 fathoms (10 to 12 metres). Ali went down and was collecting pearl shell. He sent one bag up but got no answer, when he pulled again. Upon surfacing, he found a Japanese diver from the *Vera* was on board the *Nobby*. The Japanese diver had his right arm in a bandage and was covered in a coat. His face was white due to loss of blood. He had put his arm near the compressor to reach a fallen spanner. The machine caught his sleeve and rolled his sleeve and skin up in one motion.

Kukitchi, skipper of the *Vera*, asked if Ali could take the diver to hospital on Thursday Island as the *Nobby* was faster than the *Vera*. They left at 3pm and arrived at Thursday Island about 9pm. Ali saw his boss Walter Schimafanny fishing at the wharf and called to him to get a taxi. Kukitchi and the diver went ashore in a dinghy. Ali and his crew went ashore too. That gave Ali the chance to see Carmen and the family, but the next day he was back out to sea again at 6am.

***

Ali weighed about 9 stone (57 kilograms) at the time he was a diver. The bends affected Ali from the waist down and a doctor advised him to ride a bike to build up his leg muscles. Some of the other divers, such as Vincent Dorante and Tommy Nakata are, like Ali, still around today to share their stories

But pearling was the only job Ali knew. From the age of 16 to 35 he'd been a pearl shell diver. He thought he contracted typhoid fever at Badu Island in 1951, but didn't know how he contracted it. His doctor thought he may have been bitten by a mosquito while collecting water. Ali was immediately quarantined at the Thursday Island hospital. For 4 to 6 weeks and wasn't allowed any visitors. Carmen visited him along with other nurses and sisters. That, coupled with the scare of nitrogen in his blood made Ali retire from pearling.

The following table shows the boats Ali worked on in his long life pearl shell diving.

Year/age	Lugger	Owner	Duration
14	Haku	Cleveland Pearling Company	3 months/1 season: crew
14-15	Jogen	Carpenter fleet	March – May: crew
15	Zena	Carpenter fleet	June – August: crew
15-16	Sedney	Bowden Pearling Co.	2 years: crew/cook; learnt to dive
17	Cuckoo	Bowden Pearling Co.	1 year: crew
18	Goose	Hocking Pearling Co.	1year: 2nd diver
1936/19	Penguin	Hocking Pearling Co.	1 year. 2nd diver
1937		Year off pearling	
1938/21	Pearls	Farquhar Pearling Co.	1 year. skipper, no. 1 diver
1939/22	Charm	Farquhar Pearling Co.	1 year. skipper, no. 1 diver
1940		Year off pearling	
		Ali left pearling due to the war	
1948	Nobby	Schimafanny/Van de Loo	skipper, no. 1 diver
1949	Gypsey		skipper, no. 1 diver
1950-1951	Whyalla		skipper, no. 1 diver

Wartime

We're watching on Port War Hill / Watching for ships that go by / In case there may be something, something to do with a spy /

We're watching on Port War Hill / Knowing there's no use to sigh / For there's eight

Port War Hill
public domain, attributed to Ahboo (Charlie) Ah Mat

In 1940 Australia's relations with Japan deteriorated and a defence committee met to discuss the placement of coastal guns in the Torres Strait. Port War Signal stations were established on Wednesday Island, Booby Island and Thursday Island operated and manned by the Navy. 'Port War Hill' probably refers to the base on Milman Hill on Thursday Island, which overlooked the navy refuelling tanks and wharf and provided early warning of ships coming from southern or northern ports and any enemy movements. It was also a communication point with the Port War Signal Station on Wednesday Island.

In 1940, in his year off from pearl shell diving, Ali joined the Main Roads Commission on Thursday Island. The Main Roads Commission was seeking men to work on infrastructure and capital works projects in the Torres Strait. Looking for a change from pearl shell diving, Ali decided to join and ended up working with them for about two years.

***

Ali's work gang was known as the 'flying gang' as they worked all over the Torres Strait. His overseer was Lloyd, second in charge was Lyle Graham, the foreman was Ned Penwell and the paymaster was 'Digger' Bennett. Ali made friends with three brothers, Eddie, Caverie and Simeon Sebasio, also in the flying gang.

Everyone in the gang was issued with a helmet, 50 rounds of bullets on a belt (like a bandelero), and a Lee Enfield rifle. The issuing officer told them: 'This is your second skin; wherever you go it goes too.' When Ali was told to carry it with him at all times he questioned why he should do this as he was a construction worker, not a soldier. Ali expected the soldiers to protect the workers and defend Australia. In response he was told that the workers might have to defend Australia if the Japanese invaded through the Torres Strait.

Ali and his work gang used the rifle and bullets mainly for target practice. He treated the rifle as his friend, taking it with him, never knowing when he might need it. His work gang were also ordered not to walk alone at night but to stay in groups of three or four. The concern at the time was of an invasion and it was expected that such an event would happen at night. As a part of their job, Ali and his work gang were also taught unarmed combat and self-defence in case they were attacked.

A sergeant taught them judo and one day at training he wanted to demonstrate a move. He asked Ali to attack him and throw his best punch. Ali did so and before he knew it he was flying through the air. Ali waited, watched and learned all the sergeant taught them. One day he got the opportunity to put into practice what he'd learned. The sergeant made a wrong move, Ali spotted a weakness and moved quickly, taking the sergeant offguard and throwing him to the ground. The sergeant was surprised and exclaimed, 'Ali you're a bloody bastard!!!'

***

The flying gang worked mainly on Thursday Island, Horn Island and Goode Island. One of the gang's first jobs was to build a road on Goode Island from the ocean to the fort at the side of the hill. Once that was completed they started work on the fort and two gun emplacements. The men in

Ali's work gang wrote their names on the fort when they finished the construction.

Two six-inch (21 cm) guns were shipped from mainland Australia on the *Zealandie*, a former passenger-ship-turned-troop ship. It was later sent to Darwin and while working there it was bombed and then sank. After the guns were in place they were tested by firing out towards Booby Island. Ali recalls the ground shaking when they were fired. The gang later built ammunition dumps and army huts for a camp.

The Hocking Pearling Company built a weekend retreat called *Wanetta* on Goode Island. The flying gang rebuilt the well at the back of the retreat, which was built on a natural spring at the foot of the hills. A pipeline was then

Ali working at a well, back of Wanetta, the Hocking house on Goode Island.

built from the well down to the camp. Their next task was to assist the other work gangs to rebuild the wharf and the road leading from the wharf to the fort. Ali remembers the men rising at 7am to work. Soldiers were stationed there too and worked alongside them.

While the men enjoyed working, they had to remain alert, especially at night and when they were alone. One night Ali was working late on a job, finishing cementing and smoothing the foundation for the hospital. When Ali heard a noise behind him he picked up a stone ready to throw it at whatever or whoever made the noise. He turned quickly in the direction of the noise. Stone in hand, he saw that it was his foreman, Ned Penwell. He scolded Ned and told him to make more of a noise and not to approach from behind.

On another evening Ali and some of the men were walking along the beach, looking for turtle eggs. Suddenly searchlights shone into their eyes and soldiers approached them. The soldiers questioned them and told them not to walk around there again at night.

While food was provided at a canteen wherever they worked, Ali and his work gang would often go fishing. They would fish off the wharf at Goode Island and check their fish traps for crayfish or fish. Whatever they caught was what they ate. They would sometimes carry their own cooking supplies with them, so that they could cook and eat fresh food whenever they wanted.

They had a bit of help from Smokey the dog too. Smokey belonged to Eddie Sebasio and was good at catching wild pig and deer. Ali remembered that Smokey caught a pig one day and, with the three Sebasio brothers, they enjoyed a meal of dineg wan, pig cooked in its own blood.

Overall it took about 6 to 7 months to complete work on Goode Island. During this time the men had the help of only one bulldozer and caterpiller tractor. Other than that, their equipment was basic, and it was hard work. Ali's gang was one of the last working gangs to leave Goode Island.

***

Once the work on Goode Island was completed the work gang was transferred to Thursday Island to build the gun emplacement on Milman Hill. His work gang was then moved to Horn Island where they made a barricade for the airstrip. They also extended the boat ramp on Horn Island and then went back to Thursday Island.

Many men were involved in the construction of the Horn Island airstrip. They built the airstrip with just a grader, a caterpillar tractor and a bulldozer. Ali remembers working in the bush with Tommy Anderson to make a barricade for the airstrip. They cut a bloodwood tree into four pieces, with one in the middle and another crossways. They cut wheels out of one big tree and put barbed wire on the outside of the frame. In the evening, the two men pushed the barricade onto the airstrip to prevent any planes from landing.

The fear of a Japanese invasion was not unfounded, as the Japanese bombed Horn Island several times. There is a TI legend that the Japanese didn't bomb Thursday Island because a Japanese princess was buried there. It might also have been out of respect for the many Japanese divers buried on Thursday Island.

Nonetheless, there was a lot of activity in the air, on the ground and on the water. Catalinas, or flying boats, would pass through the Torres Strait. Ships brought timber, food, bombs, guns and ammunition. Ali remembers seeing fifty planes in the air while he was working on Thursday Island. They landed at Horn Island to refuel before heading north to Port Moresby.

Ali was on Horn Island one day when he heard the air siren warning. He ran to a slit trench and heard a noise like a bumble bee. It was the Japanese planes overhead, photographing the land.

A few days later at the Thursday Island wharf, Ali was loading timber on a lugger for the Horn Island airstrip. He was on the deck of the lugger and again heard the air siren warning. He ran to the gutter at the side of the Grand Hotel, near where the Commonwealth Centre building stands today. Others thought it a good place to shelter too. By the time he ran up the wharf to the gutter he found a number of men had beaten him there.

At midday on 24 February 1942 the Japanese bombed Horn Island. A Cobra fighter plane and rocket-firing Hudson were bombed and destroyed during the attack. A building near the airstrip and the dam were damaged.

Later, Kittyhawk planes were based on Horn Island but the field was found to be too short for larger planes. So they moved the base to Higginsfield (later renamed Jacky Jacky) at Bamaga on Cape York Peninsula.

***

Most of the residents of Thursday Island and some from the outer islands were evacuated to mainland Australia. It was mostly women, children and older residents who were moved, to stay with relations on mainland Australia until the threat of an invasion had passed. In December 1941, Ali's family, Carmen senior and Carmen junior, were evacuated to Cairns on the *Ormiston*, while Ali remained on Thursday Island to work. Ali and Carmen were apart for several months, but they wrote letters to one another to keep in touch. Ali recalls Thursday Island being a quiet place after the evacuation.

The old wharf, where the office was situated, was divided into two sections. One side held foodstuffs and the other side, ammunition. The front contained fuel dumps and timber. All materials were moved by hand as there were no machines. Meat came from Bamaga (also known as Red Island) and water was accessed from Prince of Wales.

The Japanese pearl shell divers, if they had not returned to Japan, were placed in an internment camp on Thursday Island. Their families were sent to camps on mainland Australia. The camp on Thursday Island was known locally as 'Jap town'. There were three machine guns on each corner of the internment camp with about six guards posted there.

Ali summed up this period of time as exciting, yet dangerous. He recalls the attitude of some soldiers from Atherton whom he met later on. They described it as a picnic where they were paid to go fishing every day. Ali's response was 'not in my time, that was action'. He believed there was a real and immediate danger of the Japanese invading Australia.

A few days before Christmas in 1941, Ali was advised that Carmen was ill. He received permission to leave Thursday Island and went to Cairns a week before Easter in 1942. With his discharge papers he arrived in Cairns and found that Carmen was making a good recovery. Later the family moved to Mossman where Ali took up work cane cutting.

Life on the Land

Ali began work cane cutting in 1942 in the sugar industry in Queensland where he worked for about five years. In that same year, he started working with the Allied Works Council (later known as the Civil Construction Corporation [CCC]) during the off season.

In 1942, he cut cane in Mossman for George Quaid. The next season he worked for Onslow Andrews with Utan Walters. The following season he worked for Stan Andrews in Miallo, Mossman. He worked for Stan Andrews for three years before he returned to Thursday Island in July 1948, back to his life pearl shell diving. His family followed shortly afterwards.

Cane cutting was a laborious job and everyone pitched in to help. One day while playing football, a mate of Ali's jarred his wrist. The men, Ali included, helped to burn the cane. With Ali's mate unable to work, Carmen helped out too, loading the cane while he cut it. Ali remembers the sweet honey smell of the sugar cane. For his work he earned a good wage of about £45 a fortnight ($2546 in today's money).

Ali cut cane in Tully too. While there with his family the Japanese bombed Townsville. Ali and Carmen lived with their family in a house on the side of a hill. When Carmen was afraid when the bombing began, Ali reminded her they could always run and hide in the bushes on the hill.

While cane cutting in Mossman, Ali received a letter from the army to go to Cairns for a medical check up and to enrol in the army. He received notification to enrol twice. His boss at the time, Stan Andrews, who owned the farm where Ali worked, wrote back to say that Ali's contribution to the sugar industry was just as important as fighting to defend the country, and that Ali was needed on the farm. Indeed, that while the defence of the country was important, someone had to feed the Australian Army. What also helped was that Ali worked at two jobs. During the cane cutting season, he worked on the farm; during the off-season, he worked with the CCC. That way, Ali stayed on the farm till the war ended.

Ali also remembers some Italian farmers being interned during the war at camp Cowrie/Karra. When Italy broke away from Germany they were released.

***

Ali worked along the Kuranda Range (from Cairns to the Kuranda hills) from 1943 to 1944. The road had already

Ali canecutting in Mossman, 1942.

been built while his working gang maintained the road. The road was gravel, with no bitumen. After a big rain the gang had to remove stones and debris from the road and fill in any holes. There were many American soldiers who drove on the road on their way to and from their base at Mareeba. Their trucks were heavy ones, built to cross creeks and rivers.

Ali, Carmen and the family moved to Cairns. Ali now worked away from home on day jobs. Other jobs he undertook included building army nurses quarters (army huts), near the airport; the fuel pipeline to Cairns main wharf from the fuel depot; the navy depot in Grafton Street, and the gun emplacement at Brown Bay between Cairns and Yarrabah.

At that time the Palmerston and Gillies Highway were built, but these highways were only gravel roads. The men slept in camps, as they had nowhere else to sleep. Ali's work day would begin when he was picked up at Akee Street or the crossing. The work gang would drive to their work location and work throughout the day, stopping only for smoko (morning and afternoon tea) and lunch. His day ended at about 4.30 to 5.00 in the afternoon when he was dropped back home.

Ali's work gang consisted of about 5 or 6 men: three were from Darwin, having arrived after Darwin was bombed. Two of them were called George (of Greek background) and there was Tiny (so called because he was about 182cm tall). They'd come to Cairns to build the airstrip. Ali and Ned May were two other members of the work gang who used only picks and shovels to do their work.

While it wasn't necessarily very exciting work, especially after his time at sea, there was always something happening. There was news in Cairns of a Maori man who deserted a ship in Sydney. He made his way to Cairns

Carmen with baby Vicky in arms, Bonnie and Bulgai, Mossman, July 1947

undetected, but was eventually identified due to a tattoo on his body. He was a quiet person who kept to himself. He worked in Ali's gang until he was discovered. Ali and his mates were sitting down having smoko when two detectives arrived to talk to the foreman. The Maori turned his back and looked away. The detectives asked if he was an Aboriginal. When the foreman said that, no, he was a Maori, the detectives grabbed him and made arrangements to send him back to his ship in Sydney. Reflecting on the incident, Ali said, 'Once you get your body tattoed that's it; you're marked then'.

Ali recalls another day when Tiny was eating a chilli. A work mate bet Tiny that he could eat the chilli without it being hot. He must have thought that the chillies weren't hot. What he didn't know was that Tiny swallowed the chilli whole and imitated chewing movements. The other guy bit into the chilli and chewed it. At this point he

Bulgai, Bonni, Cux and Ali going to town, Mossman, 1947.

realised the chilli was very hot! His face turned red and he quickly sought something to cool his mouth. Everyone had a good laugh.

Another time this same cheeky bloke boasted that he could brew the tea the same way the stockmen in the bush did by swinging the can of billy tea around in the air. He tried to do the same thing, but the billy can and tea went flying all over the place. The next time the work gang had smoko the billy boy made the tea!

During 1945 and 1946, at war's end, Ali was still cutting cane. Stan Andrews told him the good news that the war had ended and to have the rest of the day off to go and celebrate with friends. Ali took him at his word. He stopped what he was doing and went to Mossman to celebrate. However, he continued to work with CCC and cane cutting around Cairns for a while.

Family

Island lady / Flower in your hair / Island lady / No other can compare / Your sun-kissed smile makes it all worthwhile coming home to you / When you're not around I feel let down and oh so blue / Island lady dancing cheek to cheek / Island lady / though it's just a week / Strolling hand in hand down Parade Avenue under a tropic sky / You skip and you jump then you turn around / And say I love you / Island lady / Though you're far away / Island lady / Far away and out of reach / And then I awake from this special dream / To touch you to hold you not so real as it seems / Island lady island lady / I love you

Island Lady
Henry (Seaman) Dan (Hot Music)

Ali's sometimes dangerous life at sea working on the lugger meant that the crew would be away from Thursday Island for up to six weeks, or until their food supplies ran out. When the luggers returned to Thursday Island the crew would look forward to reuniting with their families, meeting people and enjoying the entertainment of the day. Going to the picture show, the movies, and getting together for parties were the main forms of entertainment. Movies were usually held on Wednesday, Friday and Saturday nights. The picture show was then an open-air theatre, with a big Moreton Bay fig growing next to the screen. Silent films were accompanied by music and tickets cost one shilling and sixpence ($5.60 in today's money), with the balcony seats two shillings and sixpence ($9.30).

When a party was planned the ladies would bring a plate of food and the men brought soft drinks, as there was limited alcohol in those days. Everyone met at an arranged place at an agreed time and walked to the party's venue. Ali's cousin, Kitchell Ano, played the guitar and ukulele, Harry Hodges the accordion and Sollie Tolassie the mandolin. Furniture was moved around for dancing which carried on into the night, and most of the partygoers would come back the next day to help clean up.

***

It was during the off-season for trochus shell that Ali had met Carmen Bertha Villaflor. He recalls that 'she was the first woman, the first and only love for him'. They'd first met after the picture show. After the movie, Ali had gone to get some water from an old reservoir near the house where Carmen was staying. She asked him what he was doing and if he had permission to take the water. He replied yes. He recalls it being dark and that he 'didn't know her from a bar of soap'.

Carmen had come to Thursday Island with friends on holidays from Darwin. Born on 16 July 1915, Carmen grew up in Darwin. Carmen's mother was Victoria Alberleda, while her grandmother (mother's mother) was from Moa Island. Her father, Donald Villaflor, was of Philippine and Spanish-Portuguese background. Ali recalls that he may have been a pearl shell diver. Carmen was one of seven children (four girls and three boys). Carmen's parents lived in Darwin and owned land near the rice plantations at Humptydoo outside Darwin. Not much else is known of her early years in Darwin, until she took the bold step of travelling by ship to Thursday Island with a friend. Carmen stayed with Jack and Lulu Assan, friends of her family.

The next time Ali saw Carmen, she was with her friends in the main street. Ali was walking with his mate Ali Ah Mat. Ali Ah Mat said, 'Lee (their nickname for each other), there's that girl from Darwin.' Ali and Carmen walked past one another and made eye contact. He managed to say 'hello' to her the next day, when she was at the swimming pool. She had made such an impression on him that Ali said he 'should have looked before he leaped'.

Two weeks later he met her formally at a dance. A party was held at the house where Carmen was babysitting and Ali's crew had been invited. He was surprised and happy to see her there. That night, Ali says they talked 'about anything and everything'. Later, friends tried to discourage him from having a relationship with her, because she was new to town and not part of his circle of friends, but this made him even more determined to see her. The next few months were the off-season for pearling so Ali took the opportunity to court Carmen. They spent a lot of time together, but then the time came for Ali to go back to sea. He was six weeks out at sea when Carmen sent a message letting him that she was pregnant.

She sought her mother's permission for her to marry as she was under 21 at the time, the age of consent. The police magistrate, John McLean, gave permission for Ali to marry Carmen as Ali too was also under 21 and both his parents were deceased.

Ali and Carmen were married on 19 May 1936, in the Catholic Presbytery office on Thursday Island. Ali was 18 and Carmen was 20. The ceremony was performed by Father Doyle, the resident Catholic priest. They couldn't marry in a church because Ali was not Catholic, although he later converted to Catholicism when his children were growing up. Jack Assan was the best man and Lulu Assan the matron of honour. The crew of the lugger were invited to attend the wedding and about 50 to 60 guests helped them celebrate their happy day.

Ali was still working then as second diver on the *Goose*. Their wedding cost seven pounds and ten shillings (about $548.80 in today's money): a month's wages for Ali. Carmen looked after all the wedding preparations while Ali was out at sea.

Ali's boat came in the morning of their wedding day and they were married that night. There was no honeymoon, since Ali could only stay the night before leaving the next day to go back out to sea.

Ali and Carmen's plan for a family began with heartache and sorrow at the death of their first child. Although Carmen had been pregnant when they were married she lost her baby. However, not more than a year later they had a baby girl. Carmen junior was the first of the eight children Ali and Carmen senior would have together. As with all children they were to bring great happiness to Ali and Carmen and have gone on to have families of their own.

***

While Ali worked, Carmen stayed at home and ensured the home ran smoothly. They enjoyed life on Thursday Island, falling into a routine, until World War II. During December 1941, Carmen was evacuated with her daughter to Cairns, along with many others from Thursday Island. The threat of a Japanese invasion was very real and close to the northern borders of Australia. Ali remained in the Torres Strait working as a civilian construction worker, meaning that he and Carmen were separated for several months. Ali later rejoined his family in Cairns and they moved to Mossman where Ali worked cutting sugar cane. Later they moved back to Cairns.

***

Ali and Carmen's family grew rapidly. On 17 February 1944, Ali Donishio (Bulgai) was born in the Cairns Hospital. Carmen junior was about seven-years-old at the time and went to the Miallo State School. Ali junior was named after Carmen's father, Donishio and Ali senior.

A year later in 1945, Yvonne Leah (Bonnie) was born in the Mossman Hospital. She was named after Ali's sister, Leah. Two years later in 1947, Victoria Ann (Vicky) was born in the Mossman Hospital. Being a premature baby, she spent the first few weeks of her life in the hospital. She was named after Carmen's mother, Victoria who lived in Darwin.

On 24 December 1948, Christine Eve (Tina) was born at the Thursday Island Hospital. Three years later in January 1951, Sylvia Veronica (Dilly) joined the family.

Finally in 1953, their last child Paul Mario was born. He was baptised and named at the hospital. He was named after a Catholic saint.

***

Ali and Carmen moved again to the Torres Strait and began their life anew with their family, on Thursday Island. They rented a house for approximately ten pounds a year (about $518 in today's money). Shortly, after the owner decided to sell and asked for £75 (about $3518). Ali and Carmen bought their first house and land on Thursday Island.

In 1952 they demolished the existing house and built a new one. Ali and Carmen attended a meeting of the Malay Club and asked the members for assistance in building a house. The Malay Club was a friendly, social club and worked on the principle of reciprocity. Members paid

Carmen and children on a beach on Thursday Island, 1954.

£1 a month (about $28) as a membership fee. Ali says, 'They worked on the motto of you come give me a hand and I give you hand.' Members came from a Malay background and would assist one another with family and community obligations.

Victor Villaflor, Carmen's brother, helped to build the house too. After the house was built they bought a carton of beer and made kai-kai, dinner, for the workers. In return they helped other people build houses on Thursday Island. Ali still lives in his house on Hargreave Street.

By the time Ali had begun working as a labourer on the wharf. He joined as a casual worker before gaining full time employment. He was a winch driver using a steam winch, before it changed to electric, which he used to load and unload cargo from the boats. The work was often shift work from 6pm to 12am. Ali was a member of the Waterside Workers' Federation.

**

No story of Ali Drummond would be complete without telling about his beloved wife Carmen and without including the reflections of their family.

Aunty Teena (Christine Vogt) recalls this story of her mother:

> One day Mum and Dad decided to go fishing at number one reef and while they were out fishing and catching a lot of fish, Dad spotted a turtle fast (two turtles mating) floating down near them. So he said to Mum, 'Carmen roll up your line, we are going to spear a turtle'.
>
> Mum was excited and quickly rolled up her fishing line. Dad pulled up the anchor and explained to Mum that he'd be standing in the front with the turtle spear, whap. When he pointed to the left that indicated that Mum was to steer the boat to port (left) and so on.

Dad stood up front pointing left, right and straight ahead and Mum would steer the boat according to the direction given. All of a sudden Dad pointed straight ahead and mum steered straight ahead, but she also stood up so she could see.

Unfortunately, her hand accidentally turned the handle faster and poor Dad fell back and hit his head. The boat banged into the turtles and they swam away. Dad got up and looked at the turtles swimming away and swore at Mum for making a mistake. When they came home that day we heard the story at tea time about the turtle that got away and how Dad had fallen.

Aunty Dilly (Sylvia Grainger) remembers that Carmen would always wait up for the girls when they went out:

> I was about 19-years-old when I went out one evening. I'd had a few drinks and came home late. Carmen was waiting up for me and as I walked up the steps, Carmen asked me, 'Are you drunk?' 'No,' I replied. But as I walked past her I giggled.
>
> Carmen hit me on the head and I giggled again. Carmen asked me again, 'Are you drunk?' I insisted I wasn't. My sister Teena saw me and suggested going to the toilet. This was a thunderbox at the rear of the house, along a narrow concrete path leading from the house. I concentrated very hard to walk along the path but I couldn't and I erupted into fits of laughter along the way. That's only one of the times I remember my mother waiting up for us.

Vicky (Duff) remembers:

> Mum was always our number one supporter at basketball and would argue with the referee if she thought he'd

> made a wrong decision. She was a good Catholic and every year supported the Catholic Fete in October by getting a few ladies together to sew and make things for a stall that night.
>
> She didn't mind extras for lunch when our friends came around during the weekends or holidays. She loved to go fishing with Dad and they would always be back home in time for Mum to go to the TAB to have a bet. She was a strong-willed person and wouldn't hesitate to speak her mind. She still was a great Mum.

The children would often fight with each other, as siblings are prone to do. Carmen would threaten, 'You wait until your father comes home'. However, Ali rarely punished the children, as the threat alone was enough to scare them.

All the family enjoy sharing their memories of Ali and Carmen's life together. None more so than stories about fishing.

Aunty Bonnie (Yvonne Turner) tells this story:

> Back in the late fifties, Dad, Brian Muhamad (my cousin) and myself went line trawling up around the back of Entrance Island, one of the many secret spots of Dad's. It was at this sandstone bar that we were trawling. Dad was steering with Brian and I was holding the trawling line. Suddenly I got a strike, a fish biting the line, which almost pulled me overboard. I tried to hold the line.
>
> I stepped back straight on to the loop of the slack lines and that's when the trouble began. The fish decided to swim further out dragging my left leg still with the line wrapped around it and myself too. Dad's smart thinking sorted out the situation quickly.
>
> He slowed the motor, grabbed the line so I could pull my leg back into the boat and released the line.

Ali (holding nephew Joey Drummond) with Carmen, his daughters and son, Paul, 1965.

The pain was so unbearable that I nearly passed out. After about 20 minutes, Dad landed the fish and to our surprise it was a 7-feet (2.1m) sailfish, one of the first reported sailfish caught in the Torres Strait.

Aunty Dilly has her own fishing story to tell:

I remember when I was about 6 or 8 years old. This day Dad had gone out fishing. He came home with a big catch of large fish and was cleaning them on a bench near the kitchen door. Me, being Mum's pet, thought I'd get Dad's attention in some way but he ignored me completely.

So I decided to throw a temper tantrum. I started to make small whining noises, gradually getting louder and louder. This was an attempt to make him stop what he was doing and pay some attention to me. I didn't realise that Dad was in no mood to put up with my carrying on and he very casually, without a word, bent down and picked up a bucket of bloody fish water, full of scales and bloody bits, and threw the lot over me.

I stopped in the middle of my whining, having this cold, mixed bloody fish bits and scales running down me. It stopped me dead in my tracks. I couldn't cry, talk or do anything. I realised I'd finally got Dad's attention but his reaction also stunned me. This was the first and the last time I ever attempted to get my Dad's attention again.

Aunty Cux (Carmen Nunan) also has a story:

Mary Davis worked at the fish and chip shop in town and Dad would sell fish to her. One day he asked me to take the bag full of fish to her. I was tired and cranky and didn't want to go. I mumbled something under my breath and the next thing I knew the fish bag hit me. After all that I still had to take the fish to Mary Davis.

and many more:

One day Ali and his son-in-law Barry went fishing. However, what they would really do is jump in the dinghy and go to the main wharf. They'd leave the dinghy there and walk up the hill to the Grand Hotel. On one particular day Carmen was cycling on the esplanade around the front of the island and spotted the dinghy. She went home and waited for them both to return. When they got home Carmen was waiting and began questioning them. Barry quickly deserted his father-in-law and left him to face the music alone!

Ali once caught a large cod at Goode Island. When Carmen, Ali and Teena went ashore to get bait they saw a large shadow in the water. They thought it was a crocodile coming in for food but soon saw instead that it was a big fish about the size of a small dugong. They threw fish guts in the water to attract it and secured a towline around a mangrove tree. They hooked live blue fish on a towline and caught the cod. Ali pulled him in while Carmen took the slack around the tree. They hauled him in and killed the cod using a sharp rock.

They managed to lift the fish on to the bow of the boat and headed back to Thursday Island. They could not penetrate the cod's skin and had to use a small axe to scale and fillet it. They threw away the head and bone and sold the fillets to Mary Davis at the fish and chip shop for 8 pounds (3.6 kilograms).

Another favourite pastime was dragging the cast net for fish from the beach. Everyone joined in and we had lots of fun. Some of the fish we caught would be cooked for our lunch. We would often have roasted fish and numas (marinated raw fish). Yum!

Many of the family's stories are about fishing trips. On some of these trips they learnt valuable lessons.

Aunty Teena remembers this story:

I can remember after school, when I was about 10-years-old we used to come home from school, get changed into our play clothes and go out fishing with our cousins. Dad would get the boat ready and wait for us. This particular afternoon we went to Black Rock which was noted for lots of good fishing and also lots of sharks.

As we were fishing and catching a few good fish, I got a bit bored and headed for the top cabin to sit and relax. I relaxed very quickly and sat sideways on the top cabin and as I was nodding off to sleep, I slowly slipped into the deep blue saltwater. I screamed at my Dad to help me but he just yelled back to keep on swimming a bit harder. I was so frightened of sharks and the water was cold. I didn't want to get eaten by a shark today. When I got to the boat my t-shirt didn't even feel wet at all. I must have swum above the water but I remember being very upset with my Dad for not helping me. I wasn't talking with him at all on the boat.

When we got home to my mother, I yelled at her about Dad not saving me. She got an earful of abuse and I cried a lot as I hadn't wanted to cry on the boat. To this day when I see him, I still remember that time and love him for not helping me. I think it was his way to help me be independent. From that day, I was my own boss making my own decision in life. Thanks Dad.

Aunty Dilly remembers gaining her independence in relation to money:

At about 17 or 18-years-old, I left school and was changing from one job to another. I was ready to spread my wings and was learning to drive a scooter. I wanted to buy one and enquired about how much one would cost. The deposit was about $300, plus a monthly or fortnightly payment.

Having just finished working at a job and getting a pay-off I didn't have enough money to afford to buy a scooter, so I asked Dad if he would give me the amount needed and I would eventually pay him back. His answer was 'no' but he would give his name as guarantor for me. I ended up getting one of my other sisters to help me with part of the payment of the scooter. Because of this refusal on Dad's part, it has made me stand on my own two feet. I realised that if I have no money to buy anything then I would have to save to purchase the item and not count on Dad or any other person for the money. To this day I have not asked Dad for any money that I cannot payback within a certain timeframe.

Vicky, remembers that her siblings enjoyed a good childhood:

> In the late sixties, Dad had a boat called the *Karinga*. Most days he would go fishing, except on Sundays, which was our 'family day'. Dad would take the family plus one or two of our friends for a picnic on one of the many islands around Thursday Island. Wherever we went, we would either go fishing, crabbing or collecting oysters and periwinkles off the rocks.

Carmen stayed at home to look after the house and the children and was 'the disciplinarian with the children, often giving them a growling and a flogging,' Ali

Ali and Carmen's family: (front) Joey (Jessie's son), Syliva, Ali, Carmen and Sonia (Teena's daughter); (back): Jessie (Ali's sister), Paul, Teena, Murray (Teena's husband), Carmen Jnr, Geordie (Vicky's husband) and Vicky.

remembers. As Ali was the fisherman he usually threw fish water at the children to settle them down, otherwise he might become really cranky.

Carmen also became involved in the Catholic Church and ensured all her family went to church together for Sunday mass.

***

When her children were grown up and left home, Carmen looked for recreational pursuits elsewhere and was known to have a flutter on the horses and greyhounds. She would often let her grandchildren pick the names of horses she'd then bet on. At times, Carmen would win and share her winnings with her family. The most she won was a treble and double which paid $4000. She also developed a keen interest in jigsaw puzzles.

In 1977, Ali had an accident on the wharf and was nearly crushed to death between a cargo of pearl shells and a forklift carrying cases of pearl shell. This incident created a number of health problems for Ali including high blood pressure and back problems.

He retired in 1978 to pursue his interests and travel. Together, Ali and Carmen travelled to Darwin, Brisbane, Sydney, Cairns, Atherton, Elliott Heads and Bundaberg. Their sons and daughter now had families of their own and Ali and Carmen enjoyed their retirement visiting their children and grandchildren. Carmen joined Ali, fishing and travelling to the mainland visiting their children and grandchildren. While Ali was happy when plenty of fish were caught, it was Carmen who untied the knots and hooked bait on the fishing lines.

***

I remember when Grandad and Nana [Ali and Carmen] would visit us on the mainland, she often brought presents and lollies for my sisters and me. She loved to spoil us. Nana would give us a handful of five-cent coins to comb her hair while she drifted off to sleep. She would often sit at the front door of their house on Thursday Island fanning herself with an old palm-woven fan and watch for Grandad to return from selling the fish in town. I remember spending many days with Nana sitting by that door.

But Nana had her moments too. When she wanted something done and I didn't do it, she would remind me with a sharp hit! I also remember that Nana used to keep old AA size batteries (and other sizes too) by the front door to throw at the neighbours' dogs and cats when they wandered into the yard. She sometimes threw these at people too!

Carmen and Ali would sometimes have other kids at their home, some living there for a long period of time. When it was someone's birthday or a significant event, Carmen would organise a party and cook for everyone.

***

Sadly, in October 1984, at the age of 69 Carmen, passed away. She was someone who had managed a family, a home and a relationship while living a life that involved a lot of travelling and using time-consuming equipment like a kerosene refrigerator and woodfire stove. She washed clothes every day. She ensured her sons and daughters received an education, including a religious one, and looked after the other neighbourhood kids too.

Carmen had a good heart and cared for her family and the broader community. She is remembered by many people for the love and care she gave to others.

> *I can see my ancestors / Sailing on the seven seas /*
> *So many, many yumpla family just like me*
>
> Ailan Man (Seaman Dan, Bernard Fernandes, Patrick Mau & Karl Neuenfeldt) Hot Music/Control

And Now

My grandfather is a simple man who has lived an extraordinary life. He has lived through various government policies regarding the treatment of Aboriginal and Torres Strait Islander peoples, as well as through significant historical times, like the rise of the pearl shell industry in the Torres Strait. He experienced the frontline of Australia during World War II. He has lived through times of recovery and nearly died on a number of occasions. He has always lived his life with dignity and respect for others. That is why Ali is respected today, not just by his family, but by many Torres Strait Islander people, for his contribution to their history.

Grandad turns 90 in 2007 and is still going strong; remarkable for an Aboriginal and Torres Strait Islander man. His family joke is that it must be all the nitrogen in his blood from his pearling days that's 'preserved' him. Grandad's journey now is a simpler one than in his busy past; he keeps on fishing and bowling and travelling between TI and Brisbane.

**

On Anzac Day, 25 April 1999, he was awarded the Civilian Service Medal on Thursday Island. The Federal Member for Leichhardt in north Queensland presented the award to Ali for his wartime service on the Torres Strait Islands, working for the Civil Construction Corporation. He was nominated by his daughter Sylvia for the Civilian Service Medal (1939–1945). The Civilian Service Medal recognises service in civilian organisations, the members of which served in support of the Australian war effort on the home front during World War II. Fifty nine years after that service he was being recognised. This is one of the many awards he's received in the later years of his long life. In that time, he's been a pearl shell diver, pearl shell skipper, wartime construction worker, cane cutter, wharf labourer, fisherman, community elder, family man and representative sportsman. Ali Drummond's story is part of the history of the Torres Strait.

Today, Ali is a respected elder and recognised across Australia. He's a Cultural Ambassador for Thursday Island and the Torres Strait, educating non-Aboriginal and Torres Strait Islander peoples about Aboriginal and Torres Strait Islander culture, which assists greatly in the role of reconciliation. In his retirement, his two great passions are playing and competing in lawn bowls and fishing, along with doing volunteer work for the community.

***

Ali started playing lawn bowls in the early 1970s. This began as a bet between two of his friends. One day when Ali was coming home from fishing in his dinghy, he found Bob Mackney, the police sergeant, and Arnie Duffield watching him. Arnie made a bet with Bob that he wouldn't be able to get Ali to play lawn bowls. Bob approached Ali to come and try a game of lawn bowls the next Saturday, men's day at the club. Ali thought long and hard about this because he couldn't see the attraction of the game. However, on the Saturday, Ali turned up at the club to try a game. Bob won the bet, and Ali enjoyed the game so much that he came back, again and again.

Before Ali began playing lawn bowls he'd thought it was a sport for older people but he soon realised that it was a game for both young and old. Since joining the Thursday Island Bowls Club in 1970 he's won numerous trophies, including two A-Grade singles, mixed pair and triplets. He's played international competition at the Arafura Games in May 1995 (playing the men's pairs) and in May 1997 (playing the men's singles), representing Queensland/ North Queensland. He plays when he is on holidays in Queensland at Atherton, Mareeba, Yungaburra, west Cairns and Cleveland. He has also represented Thursday Island against Weipa and various bowls clubs in Cairns. He earned the nickname 'Silver Fox' from Des Murphett for his silver hair and crafty sportsmanship; he's reputedly as cunning as a fox when he plays.

He won several club championships including the A-Grade Singles titles in 1986 and 1989. Since 1995, he's played at Cleveland Bowls Club and against other surrounding clubs from the Sunshine Coast to the Gold

Ali and his daughters, Vicky, Teena and Bonnie during the NAIDOC Sportsperson of the Year award, Broome, 1998.

Coast. Since 1996 he's been a regular player in the Redlands area, where he's popular as a good and competitive player. He's often played in the Strawberry Festival competition.

In 1986, Ali became a life member of the TI club. In his more than 20 years there, he's been Vice President and a committee member and helped with voluntary bar work and working bees.

In 1998, Ali was awarded the Australia Day award for the Sportsperson of the Year by the Torres Shire Council

Warren Entsch (Federal member for Leichardt) and Ali at the presentation of Ali's Civilian Service Medal, ANZAC Day, 1999.

on Thursday Island. His grandchildren accepted the award on his behalf as he was in Cleveland playing bowls. He also received the 1998 National Aboriginal and Islander Day of Observance Committee (NAIDOC) Sportsperson of the Year Award at a national ceremony in Broome.

He's introduced the game to his family and now has three daughters and a son who play; two daughters play competitively at A- and B-grade level. Ali's athletic skill as a diver has translated in later life into the tact, agility, good sportsmanship and competitive spirit that's the equal of any sportsperson.

***

Ali's other great passion takes him back to the water. He started fishing at an early age, and kept fishing while he worked on the pearling luggers. That passion was shared by Carmen and continued throughout his life together. Nowadays, he goes fishing Monday to Friday in the mornings, and sometimes on the weekends. His grandchildren often go with him. He has a number of 'secret spots' and often gets asked how he remembers where they are. He replies with a cheeky twinkle in his eye, that he 'remembers the location of his "secret spot" by marking it with a cross!'

***

As well as his volunteer work at the Lawn Bowls Club, Ali's been involved in the local community clubs, in particular with the Buffalo and Lions Club of Thursday Island. He joined the Buffalo Club in about 1953. Arthur Filewood introduced Ali and a few others to the club which was a brotherhood club, having a social gathering once a fortnight. When Ali came home from fishing, Carmen would prepare everything for Ali to get ready and attend the Buffalo Club meetings in John Street. They also held Christmas parties for members and their families. The club was disbanded when their secretary passed away.

Ali with his son Paul and Kamahl at the presentation of Ali's Senior Australian of the Year award, 1999.

Bob Mackney also introduced Ali to the Lions Club. A lot of business people were involved in the club, in particular with activities to clean up the Island. Ali was a regular member for seven years and received a seven-year attendance badge. The Lions Club held Christmas parties and ladies' nights. They would have dinner at the Federal Hotel. Ali remembers donating a 21 pound (9.5 kilograms) trevally to the club for a raffle.

***

And Now

Ali's awards. Ali holds his Senior Australian of the Year award, 1999; grand-daughter Parina (left) holds Ali's Civilian Service Medal (1939–1945); and grand-daughter Carmen holds the Australia Day Award for Sportsperson of the Year, Torres Strait Council, 1998. On the table is the NAIDOC Sportsperson of the Year award, 1998.

Ali's advice is now much sought after. He has intimate knowledge of the waters of the Torres Strait from his former years as a pearl shell diver and later as a fisherman. As one of the few remaining pearl shell divers of his time, his contribution to the history of the Torres Strait is respected, and his knowledge shared for the benefit of the community.

The Queensland Fisheries Department and Commonwealth Scientific Industrial Research Organisation (CSIRO) have both consulted with him in relation to pearl shell diving and the migration of Torres Strait marine life like turtles and crayfish. Even the medical fraternity have inquired about the effects of the bends and staging. After a death at Cowal Creek (Injinoo), the Magistrate consulted Ali on the effects of the bends in determining a cause of death for a death certificate.

In the 1990s a Japanese television crew interviewed him about pearling in the Torres Strait. The Japanese television crew told him that Thomo-san, his mentor, was still alive and living in Japan at the time.

Between 1999 and 2000, Ali contributed his story and photos to a pearling exhibition at the Museum of Tropical Queensland in Townsville. Titled 'Sugar, Shops and Pearls', the exhibition portrays the colourful and courageous stories about labour and settlement, and shows how people from other nations have added their cultures to the heritage of north Queensland.

Ali featured in the Peoplescape Exhibition, a Centenary of Federation project held in 2001, which celebrated the contribution that many have made to Australian history. The figure representing Ali was installed on the lawns of Parliament House in November 2001, along with many other notable Australian identities.

Ali is featured in the inaugural Lonely Planet guidebook *Aboriginal Australia and the Torres Strait Islands* which was launched in July 2001. The article titled 'Grandad's memories of Pearlshells and Japanese bombs' tells of Ali's experiences working during World War II and the Japanese bombing raids in the Torres Strait. He further describes his experiences diving for pearl shell and the dangers he encountered.

In 2002, Ali featured in the *Discover Queensland* program 'The Inside Guide to the State Outside', a part of the Queensland Heritage Trails network by the Queensland Museum.

***

Vicky, Ali and Sylvia enjoying a game of lawn bowls, Cleveland, February 1999.

When not involved in bowling, fishing, doing volunteer work or advising others, Ali's other interests include reading and collecting *Phantom* comics and completing word puzzles. Ali loved to read *Phantom* comics before the war, and he introduced his family and grandchildren to reading and collecting them. He likes to do word puzzles to keep him mentally active.

Ali said that he had 'no goals or plans'. He just lives day by day and looks forward to the future. He said, 'that's probably why you live so long'. He lived through the Depression and has the 'save' mentality. Each morning he plans what he's going to have for dinner that night. He looks forward to the future and to the future of his children, grandchildren, great-grandchildren and great great-grandchildren.

A family reunion in 2007 will bring together all members of the extended family to celebrate Ali's life and the diversity of his immediate and extended family. Ali's story continues.